African Myths and Egyptian Gods

A Captivating Guide to African Mythology and Gods of Ancient Egypt

Free Bonus from Captivating History
(Available for a Limited time)

Hi History Lovers!

Now you have a chance to join our exclusive history list so you can get your first history ebook for free as well as discounts and a potential to get more history books for free! Simply visit the link below to join.

Captivatinghistory.com/ebook

Also, make sure to follow us on Facebook, Twitter and Youtube by searching for Captivating History.

Contents

Part 1: African Mythology

Captivating Myths of Gods, Goddesses, and Legendary Creatures of Africa

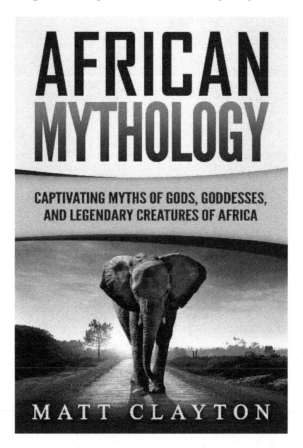

Introduction

The continent of Africa is home to fifty-four countries that together harbor over three thousand cultures, each with their own ways of life and each with their own stories. Some of these stories have their origins in the folk beliefs of people native to their particular region, while others were imported from or influenced by cultures from elsewhere who settled in Africa.

A great number of African folktales have been transmitted orally from person to person down through the ages, but since the nineteenth century, many stories have been written down and transmitted to audiences beyond the boundaries of the cultures that created them. One important—and tragic—conduit for the transmission of these stories beyond African shores was the European slave trade. Captured Africans who were brought to the Americas and the Caribbean fought to keep alive what they could of their home cultures, and this included their folktale traditions.

African folktales come in many different types. Some are myths explaining the origins of things, while others are tales of heroes with supernatural abilities. Animal stories are many and varied, and they usually involve some kind of trickster who uses his wiles to get out of sticky situations and sometimes into them. There are also cautionary tales explaining why it is important to behave well and treat others with respect, while other stories have a style and shape similar to that of a fairy tale.

This current collection presents ten stories, each taken from a different culture. As such, this book is but a small taste of the variety in the stories that African peoples have to tell and makes no claim to being in any way representative.

The first section of the book deals with the exploits of animal tricksters. Kwaku Anansi, the spider (Ghana); Nwampfundla, the hare (Mozambique; and the redoubtable Frog (Angola) all work either for themselves or for someone else, trying to get something of value from a powerful being while trying (and sometimes failing) to avoid consequences to themselves and others.

Hero tales fill the second section of the book. The first two stories, from Angola and South Africa, respectively, deal with male protagonists who, in the typical way of heroes, have supernatural births and supernatural abilities, who go out seeking adventure, and who struggle against monstrous beings that would seek to destroy them. The final story—also from South Africa—departs from the supernatural hero trope and instead presents the tale of an exceptionally observant and wise little girl who is able to save herself and her sister from a group of murderous men.

Stories from Kenya and Nigeria present moral lessons to be learned. These cautionary tales provide lessons about treating others with respect and about the dangers of greed.

The last two stories show the influence of Islam and Arab culture on African peoples. The first of these stories is from Eritrea and involves the character of Abunawas, an important Arab poet whose fictionalized persona became the hero of many folktales. The second is a fairy tale from Libya, which shows the influence of Arab storytelling in the way it resembles many of the tales in the *Arabian Nights* collection.

"African folklore" as an umbrella term is really quite inadequate as a description for the stories told by African peoples. Each of the stories in this book—and the thousands of others created and told by the myriad African cultures—is influenced by the traditions and religions practiced by their creators and by the environments in which those creators lived. These stories also represent living traditions of storytelling, traditions that have survived colonialist rapacity and the vicissitudes of modern society, and that still have new things to tell us every time we listen to them.

Part I: Animal Tricksters

How Spider Bought the Sky God's Stories *(Ashanti, Ghana)*

Kwaku Anansi, the spider, is the primary trickster in West African folklore. Stories about Anansi originated in Ghana, but when Ghanaian natives were taken abroad as slaves, the stories went with them, entering into the folklore of their descendants in the United States and the Caribbean.

The story about Anansi retold below has two particularly interesting features. One is the concept of the ownership of stories, which is common in many traditional societies. In these societies, if one wishes to tell a story owned by another person, one first must get permission to do so. Here, the stories all originally belonged to Nyankonpon, the Sky God, who asks a hefty and practically impossible price for them, but once Anansi meets the god's price, the stories become his.

The other feature is the role played by Anansi's wife, Aso. Most animal tricksters in other cultures tend to work alone: for example, Coyote in Indigenous North American lore, or Nwampfundla, the hare, in stories from the Ronga people, one of which is told below. In the story of how Anansi bought all the stories from the Sky God, Anansi relies on his wife's good advice to help him play the tricks necessary to get the items demanded by Nyankonpon, making the success of that project a team effort.

There was a time when all stories belonged to Nyankonpon, the Sky God. Kwaku Anansi, the spider, thought to himself, "It is not fair that the Sky God should have all the stories. I mean to see whether I can get them from him."

Anansi went up to Heaven. He went before Nyankonpon and said, "I want to buy all your stories. How much will I have to pay for you to sell them to me?"

Nyankonpon laughed and said, "Anansi, you are just one small creature. Many great men have tried to buy my stories. Whole cities of people have tried to buy my stories. No one has ever succeeded. What makes you think you will be able to meet my price?"

"Oh, I think I'll be able to meet it," said Anansi. "Just tell me what you want."

"Very well," said Nyankonpon. "If you want to buy my stories, you must bring me Onini, the python; Osebo, the leopard; Mmoatia, the fairy; and Mmoboro, the hornets. Bring me all of these things, and the stories will be yours."

Anansi went home and told his wife, Aso, that he had made a bargain with the Sky God to buy all his stories. "First I must bring him Onini, the python," said Anansi. "Have you any advice about how I should go about capturing him?"

"Oh, yes," said Aso. "This is what you must do: get the branch of a palm tree and some string creeper, and bring them down to the river."

"Ah! I know what to do now," said Anansi, and so he went out and got a long palm branch and some string creeper, and as he walked down to the river, he pretended to be having a conversation with his wife.

"He is not as long as this palm branch," Anansi said in his own voice.

"No, indeed," Anansi said in Aso's voice. "He is much longer than that."

"You lie," Anansi said in his own voice. "There is no way he is even this long."

As Anansi got closer to the river, Onini, the python, heard the conversation. He slithered over to Anansi and said, "What are you arguing about?"

"My wife and I had an argument about whether you are longer than this palm branch. She thinks you are longer, but I think she is wrong."

Onini said, "Bring the branch here, and we can measure to see who is right."

Anansi put the branch down on the ground, and Onini stretched himself out beside it. Quick as a wink, Anansi took the string creeper and tied Onini to the palm branch.

"Caught you!" said Anansi. "Now I shall bring you to the Sky God, and he will have to sell me all his stories."

Anansi brought the python up to Heaven and showed him to Nyankonpon. "Here is Onini, the python, the first part of my payment."

Nyankonpon looked at the python, who was tied to the palm branch. He reached out and touched the python and said, "I accept this as the first part of your payment. Bring me the rest, and my stories will be yours."

Anansi went home and told Aso how he had captured the python. "I think I shall capture the hornets next," said Anansi. "Have you any ideas about how I might do that?"

"Oh, yes," said Aso. "This is what you must do: find a gourd and a plantain leaf. Fill the gourd with water, and you may use those things to capture the hornets."

"Ah! I know what to do now," said Anansi, and he went out and found a gourd and a plantain leaf. He filled the gourd with water and then went looking for the hornets. Soon enough, he came upon a whole swarm of hornets. He took the plantain leaf and covered his head with it, then splashed the hornets with water from the gourd.

"Oh, dear, it is raining!" said Anansi to the hornets. "Would you like a place to shelter from the rain, Hornets? I have this nice plantain leaf, but I see you have no shelter. Come and sit inside my gourd until it is dry."

"Thank you!" said the hornets, and they all flew into the gourd. As soon as the last one had entered, Anansi plugged the mouth of the gourd. "Caught you!" he said. "Now I shall bring you to the Sky God, and he will have to sell me all his stories."

Anansi brought the hornets up to Heaven and showed them to Nyankonpon. "Here is Mmoboro, the hornets, the second part of my payment."

Nyankonpon looked at the gourd full of hornets. He reached out and touched the gourd and said, "I accept this as the second part of your payment. Bring me the rest, and my stories will be yours."

Anansi went home and told his wife how it had gone with the hornets. "Now I have to capture Osebo, the leopard," said Anansi. "You give me such good advice; what should I do to capture Osebo?"

"Go and dig a deep hole," said Aso.

"Yes! That is the very thing," said Anansi. "I know what to do now."

Anansi went out and looked for the leopard's tracks. When he found a place he thought a leopard was likely to visit, he dug a deep hole and covered it with banana and plantain leaves. Then he went home.

In the morning, Anansi went back to the hole. He looked over the lip of the hole and saw the leopard there.

"Help me!" cried the leopard. "Help me! I have fallen into this pit, and I can't get out again."

"Oh, you poor thing!" said Anansi. "That must be very wretched indeed for you."

"Indeed, it is," said the leopard. "Please, won't you help me get out?"

"I could do that," said Anansi, "but I bet you'll just eat me right up for my pains."

"No, no!" said the leopard. "I won't eat you, I promise! Just help me out of here, and I'll go my own way and you'll go yours."

"Very well, I'll help you," said Anansi.

Anansi got two long sticks and some string creeper. "Here, put your paws over these sticks, two in front and two in back," said Anansi. "Then I'll use the sticks to pull you up."

When the leopard put his paws over the sticks, Anansi tied them tightly with the creeper.

"Caught you!" said Anansi. "Now I can bring you to the Sky God, and he will have to sell me all his stories."

Anansi brought the leopard to Heaven and showed him to Nyankonpon. "Here is Osebo, the leopard, the third part of my payment."

Nyankonpon looked at the leopard, who was tied by his paws to the sticks. He reached out and touched the leopard and said, "I accept this as the third part of your payment. Bring me the rest, and my stories will be yours."

Anansi went home and told his wife how things had gone with the leopard. "Only one payment remains," said Anansi, "and I already know how I will get it. Please, Aso, will you make me some pounded yams?"

"Yes, I certainly will," said Aso, and off she went to cook the yams.

While Aso was busy preparing the yams, Anansi took some wood and carved an *akua,* a wooden doll with a flat face. He made it so that the head would move when pulled with a string. Then Anansi went to a tree and collected a great deal of sticky sap, which he spread all over the doll's body.

"My wife, are the yams ready?" said Anansi when the doll was done.

"Yes, they are," said Aso. "Come and take them."

Anansi took the yams Aso had made and put some of them into the hands of the doll. Then he took the doll to a tree where he knew fairies lived. Anansi hid himself in a nearby bush, with one hand holding onto the string connected to the doll's head. Sure enough, a fairy came along and saw the doll there with its hands full of delicious yams.

"Akua, may I share your yams with you?" said the fairy.

Anansi pulled the string, and the doll nodded its head.

"Thank you!" said the fairy. The fairy reached out her right hand to take the yams, but her hand stuck to the sap on the doll. Then she took her left hand and tried to remove the right one, but her left hand stuck as well. The fairy pushed at the doll with her right foot, but this was no help. It was stuck fast to the sap on the doll's body, and her left foot was stuck too as soon as she tried to use that one to remove the right foot.

When the fairy was completely stuck to the doll, Anansi came out from behind the tree and tied the fairy up. "Caught you!" said Anansi. "Now I can bring you to the Sky God, and he will have to sell me all his stories."

Anansi brought the fairy to Heaven and showed her to Nyankonpon. "Here is Mmoatia, the fairy, the fourth and last part of my payment."

Nyankonpon looked at the fairy, who was tied to the doll. He reached out and touched the fairy and said, "I accept this as the fourth and last part of your payment. You have done what many great men have failed to do. You have done what whole cities have failed to do. You have met my price, and now my stories are yours. From now on, whenever someone tells a story, they must say, 'This is Anansi's story.'"

And this is why all stories are Anansi stories and why all stories belong to the Spider.

Nwampfundla and the Elephant *(Ronga, Mozambique)*

This story about Nwampfundla, the hare, is retold from a set collected in the early twentieth century by the Reverend Herbert L. Bishop, a member of the South African Association for the Advancement of Science. Bishop recorded these stories as they were told to him by Samuel Mabika, who Bishop describes as "a great warrior [in his youth and] a man of considerable importance in his tribe."

Nwampfundla uses his tricksterish wiles to get things for himself that otherwise are forbidden and to make fools of creatures who are more powerful than he is. However, he does not get away completely scot-free; Nwampfundla often has to pay a price for his trickery.

In his notes to the stories he collected, Bishop states that the word "nwa" is used as the equivalent of "Mr." The name "Nwampfundla" therefore literally means "Mr. Hare."

As everyone knows, the lion is the great chief of all the animals. Every animal in the bush recognizes him as king. Even the elephant knows that the lion is chief, despite the elephant being much larger by far. Whenever the lion strolls by, all the animals say, "Hail, O Chief!" as he passes.

Like any good chief, the lion also has many servants and advisors to help him. One of these servants was Nwampfundla, the hare.

Wherever the lion went, Nwampfundla went with him. Whatever the lion told Nwampfundla to do, he would do.

One day, the lion said, "I think we should go somewhere else. Come with me."

And so all the animals who were servants of the chief made ready to leave. They collected all their belongings and things they would need for the journey. When the lion said, "Let us go," all the animals went with him.

The animals walked along, following the lion. It was a great procession, for the lion had many, many servants. They walked and walked until they came to a place that had a tree full of delicious fruit. Since the day was almost over, some of the animals went to the lion and said, "O Chief, we should stop here for the night. Look, there is a tree full of delicious fruit. This would be a good place for us to stop and a good place for us to spend the night."

The lion looked at the tree. He said, "Yes, I agree. This is a good place to stop and spend the night. But the fruit of the tree is only for me. No one else is to eat it. The rest of you can look about for other things to eat, but this fruit is for me."

The animals put down the things they had been carrying. They spread out their sleeping mats and made ready to spend the night. But Nwampfundla went to the lion's chief advisors and said, "I would like to speak to you about something."

"Yes, we will listen, Nwampfundla," the advisors said.

"Well," said Nwampfundla, "I am concerned about this fruit tree, the one with the fruit that our chief said we are not to touch."

"What about it?"

"Well, I don't want to get into trouble because of it," said the hare. "If someone should go and steal all the fruit while the rest of us are sleeping, surely I will be accused. Everyone will say, 'That Nwampfundla, he thinks he can get away with anything, even stealing all the lion's fruit.'"

"Why should anyone say that?" said the advisors.

"Oh, I just have this thought that they might," said the hare. "But I know how we can prevent any trouble on my account. You know that big mortar we brought for stamping corn? I'll lie down here, and you can turn the mortar upside down on top of me. That way if the fruit goes missing, everyone will know that someone else did it because I will have been shut up in the mortar all night."

The advisors laughed, but they agreed to shut Nwampfundla up in the mortar. The hare lay down on the ground, and the advisors turned the mortar upside down on top of him. Soon the camp became quiet, and all the animals went to sleep.

Once the hare was certain all the others were sleeping, he cautiously lifted up one edge of the mortar and peeped out. He looked this way and that, and everywhere he looked he saw only sleeping animals. When he saw that everyone was asleep, he crawled out from under the mortar as quietly as he could. He went over a little way to where there was a basket. He stood listening, making sure no one had heard or seen him. When he felt safe, he picked up the basket, then stopped again to listen. But none of the other animals stirred because they had eaten so well of the fruit from the other trees that the lion said they could have.

Nwampfundla went over to the lion's special tree. Holding the basket, he began to climb. He went a little way, then stopped to listen. Then he went another little way, then stopped to listen. In this way, he went all the way up the trunk and into the branches where the fruit was. When he reached the fruit, he began to eat it, and every time he finished one of the fruits, he put the stone into his basket.

Having eaten his fill of the fruit, the hare climbed quietly down the tree. Then he went to where the elephant was sleeping and hung the basket full of fruit stones behind the elephant's ear. Then he went back over the mortar, climbed underneath it, and went to sleep.

In the morning, the animals awoke and stretched in the sun. They talked among themselves as they packed up their things, making ready to continue their journey. They heard a scratching sound from inside the overturned mortar, and the hare's voice coming faintly from inside it, saying, "Please let me out! The sun is up, and I want to see the light!"

"Oh, right," said one of the advisors. "I almost forgot we put the hare under that last night."

The advisor went over and let Nwampfundla out from under the mortar. After he yawned and stretched in the sunlight, Nwampfundla went over to the lion. "Good morning, O Chief!" he said. Then he looked over at the fruit tree and said, "Look at that! I told you it was true. I told you someone would eat all the fruit you said was yours. That's why I had your advisors put me under that big mortar during the night. I didn't want to be accused."

The lion looked at the tree and saw that all the fruit had indeed been eaten. "Who did this?" he roared. "Who disobeyed me and ate all my fruit?"

All the animals quaked in fear.

"Come here and stand before me," said the lion. "Tell me who did this."

The animals all came to stand before the lion, but no one could tell him who had eaten the fruit. Then the hare came and stood in front of the lion. "If it please you, O Chief," he said, "I propose a test to see which of us stole the fruit. May I tell you my test?"

"Yes," said the lion. "Tell me."

"Very well," said the hare, "but first you must tell the animals that they have to help me."

"You all heard what the hare said," said the lion, "and that is my command, that you help him. Now, hare, tell us your plan."

"Well, first we dig a big, long pit," said the hare, "and then everyone has to jump over it. That way we will discover who took the fruit."

The animals all helped to dig the pit, and when it was ready, Nwampfundla showed them where they should jump. The lion said, "I am the chief, so therefore I jump first."

The lion jumped over the pit. Nothing happened.

Then the hare jumped. Nothing happened.

Then the leopard jumped, and nothing happened. One by one, all the animals jumped over the pit, but they were still no closer to finding out who had taken the lion's fruit.

Finally it was the elephant's turn, and he was the last one left. He jumped over the pit, and when he landed on the other side, the basket of fruit fell down from behind his ear. All the fruit stones fell out of the basket and scattered on the ground.

Nwampfundla said, "Look! We have caught the thief! See? He had a basket full of the fruit stones. The elephant is the one who ate all that fruit."

"How could I have eaten all that fruit?" said the elephant. "Look at me. I can't climb trees at all. I didn't take that fruit, not one bit of it."

The animals didn't believe the elephant. Then Nwampfundla said, "Shame on you, for stealing the king's fruit."

The lion said, "Let the elephant be killed!"

The other animals fell upon the elephant and killed him. The king gave Nwampfundla a big piece of the elephant's flesh and told the hare to carry it. And so the animals all resumed their journey with their king, and Nwampfundla staggered along behind them, carrying a big piece of the elephant's flesh.

Now, the hare was a very small animal, and the piece of elephant's flesh that he carried was very big, and soon the hare became tired. He started lagging behind the other animals. Nwampfundla also was very sad because the elephant had been killed even though he had done nothing wrong.

Nwampfundla walked behind the other animals, crying and feeling sorry for himself and saying, "The elephant didn't eat any of the lion's fruit, but they killed him anyway."

The animals walking in front of the hare heard him crying. They heard him talking to himself, but they couldn't understand what he was saying.

Suddenly, the lion stopped. He turned around and saw Nwampfundla lagging behind all the other animals. The lion called to the hare and said, "Nwampfundla! Come up here and walk next to me. You are lagging too far behind."

"O my Chief," said the hare, "I want to do your bidding, but I must carry this heavy piece of meat. I am very small, and the piece of meat is very big. I cannot walk fast enough to be beside you and carry this piece of meat at the same time."

The lion had the piece of meat divided into two pieces. He told one of the larger animals to carry the big piece and gave the smaller piece to Nwampfundla. Then the lion and his entourage resumed their journey.

It was not long before Nwampfundla again was staggering along behind all the other animals, crying and talking to himself.

"Oh, it is such a sad thing that they killed the elephant. He didn't do anything wrong. He didn't eat any of the fruit. I'm the one that ate it, but he's the one that was killed."

Again the lion turned and saw Nwampfundla struggling along on the path, crying and talking to himself. The lion said, "Nwampfundla! Why do you stagger along so far behind everyone? You must come and walk closer to me."

Nwampfundla answered, "O my Chief, I want to do your bidding, but this piece of meat is too heavy for me since I am only a very small animal."

The lion took the piece of meat from the hare and gave it to another animal to carry. Then he gave his assegais, his bundle of javelins, to Nwampfundla, saying, "Here, you must carry my assegais. They are not too heavy. Also you must walk in front of me."

Nwampfundla took the assegais and walked in front of the lion. While he walked, he began singing the song that he had made about the elephant. "Oh, they killed the elephant, even though he did nothing wrong. They killed him, even though he ate none of the lion's fruit. They killed the elephant, but it was I who ate the fruit."

This time the lion heard what the hare was saying. "What is that you are singing about? Was it really you that ate all my fruit from my special tree?"

"Yes, I ate the fruit, my Chief, but the elephant paid the price for it, and I am very sorry about that."

Then the lion became very angry. "So, it was you the whole time!" He turned to the other animals and roared, "Catch that thief!"

Nwampfundla ran away as fast as his legs could carry him, with all the other animals chasing along behind. But no matter how fast the other animals ran, none of them could catch Nwampfundla. Soon the hare noticed a hole in the ground, so he dove into it. The animals saw him go in. They went back to the lion and said, "That rascal went down this hole. What shall we do with him now?"

"Find a way to get him out," said the lion.

The animals went into the bush and found a good, long stick. They cut the stick to have a hook at one end, then they took the stick back to the hole. They put the stick down the hole and began to fish around with it. The hook caught Nwampfundla by the leg, but the hare only laughed and said, "Well, aren't you clever, putting a stick down the hole and catching only a root! You'll never get me that way!"

The animals took the stick out of the hole and put it down again, and this time it hooked itself around a root. When Nwampfundla saw that the stick was hooked on a root, he began to cry and scream. "Oh, no! You have hooked me by the leg! What will I do now?"

All the animals thought they had caught Nwampfundla for sure. They pulled and pulled on the stick, but it would not budge. The lion came and helped too, and again they pulled. They all pulled as hard as they could, and finally the root broke, sending all the animals falling backward on top of one another.

The lion was enraged. "You scoundrel! You rascal! When I catch you, I will have you skinned and chopped up for my dinner!"

Then the lion turned to the other animals and told them to try again. The animals put the stick down the hole, and the hook caught on the hare's leg. But when the hare laughed, the animals thought, "We must have caught another root. Surely the hare would not laugh if we had hooked him."

The animals removed the stick from the hole, then put it down again. This time they hooked another root, and Nwampfundla began to cry and beg for mercy. "Aha!" said the animals. "This time we've really got him." They pulled and pulled and pulled on the root until it broke, sending all the animals falling backward on top of one another.

The lion was even more angry than before that the hare had tricked them yet again. He roared out all the terrible things he wanted to do when he finally caught the hare, and his anger was so great that all the animals were very much afraid of him. But Nwampfundla sat in his hole, listening to the lion rage on and on, laughing and saying, "Yes, you do go on about what you will do to me, but first you have to catch me! And you cannot do that, for I, Nwampfundla the hare, am the greatest of all the animals!"

Finally, the lion and the other animals got tired of listening to the hare laugh at them. "Fine," said the lion. "If he thinks he's so great for having gone down that hole, he can stay there forever. Find grass, and plug up this end of the hole. Make it so that he cannot get out. That will teach him to make sport of me."

The animals did as the lion bid them. They took a great quantity of grass and shoved it into the hole. They packed the grass in very tightly, so that the hare could not get out. Then the lion and the other animals resumed their journey.

When the animals had gone, Nwampfundla went to the grass and tried to pull it away so that he could get out. He pulled and he pulled and he pulled, but no matter what he did, the grass stuck fast. The animals had packed it in so tightly that there was no way the hare could remove it. He was stuck inside that hole for good.

Nwampfundla sat inside the hole feeling very sorry for himself. After a while, he began to feel hungry. He got hungrier and hungrier, until at last he ate one of his own ears. This satisfied him for a time, but after a while, he became hungry again. He tried to ignore the hunger, but at last it was too strong, so he ate one of his own legs.

More time passed, and soon Nwampfundla found himself becoming thirsty. He tried and tried not to think about it, but finally he took one of his eyes out and ate it, thinking to quench his thirst with the tears that were inside it.

After Nwampfundla had eaten his ear, his leg, and his eye, there came a great storm with much wind. The wind blew so strongly that it blew the grass plug out of the hole. When the storm passed, Nwampfundla realized he could see the opening of the hole. He crept very carefully up to the entrance, and he looked around. There was no one to be seen, so he crept out of the hole.

In a nearby tree, there was a beehive. Nwampfundla took some of the wax and used it to fashion two little horns. He stuck the horns on his head and limped off to the lion's home.

The king saw the hare come into the kraal, the fenced village where the lion lived with his servants and advisors. The lion asked the other animals who this stranger was. "Oh, that must be Nwampfundla, the hare," said the animals, "the one who gave you so much trouble."

"Nonsense," said the hare. "Did this Nwampfundla have only one ear? Did he have only three legs? Did he have only one eye? Did he have horns on top of his head?"

The animals all had to admit that Nwampfundla did not have those things.

"Well, of course he didn't," said the hare. "How could he? I am a special hare from a special society of hares. We all have one ear, one eye, three legs, and horns on our heads, and there are precious few of us. You are privileged to have seen me at all, for I can run faster with three legs than any other animal can run with four, and I see farther and hear better than animals with two eyes and two ears. I am the best servant any chief could ever wish for."

The lion was very pleased by what the hare had said. "If you really can do all those things," said the lion, "then please stay on and be my servant. A chief needs servants who can do such marvelous things as you can."

And so it was that Nwampfundla once again became a servant to the lion.

The Daughter of the Sun and Moon *(Ambundu, Angola)*

Na Kimanaueze is an important culture hero of the Ambundu people of Angola. He is the subject of a cycle of hero stories and a character in hero stories about his son and grandson. The stories originally were transmitted orally, but they were first recorded in writing by European anthropologists in the nineteenth century.

In this story, the younger Kimanaueze wants to marry the daughter of the Sun and Moon, and although he is a major character and the person around whom the story revolves, he himself does not do the work of securing the young woman's hand in marriage. That task falls to the trickster Frog, who finds a way to go back and forth between Heaven and Earth and to convince the Sun and Moon that their daughter should be the younger Kimanaueze's bride.

We see in this story some important aspects of Ambundu culture surrounding courtship and marriage. The younger Kimanaueze must prove that he is worthy to marry the young woman by paying an appropriate bride-price, and with each installment that Frog brings up to Heaven, the young woman's family provides a good meal for their guest, not realizing that it is Frog and not the suitor who has been visiting their home.

The great hero and chieftain Na Kimanaueze had a son named Kimanaueze kia Tumb' a Ndala. When the son of Na Kimanaueze had grown to manhood, his father came to him and said, "It is time we found a wife for you. There are many beautiful girls in our village. Choose one, and we will go to her family and ask whether you might marry her."

But the son of Na Kimanaueze said, "I will not marry any of the girls in our village."

"Very well," said Na Kimanaueze. "Perhaps we can go to the next village and find a wife for you there."

"No, that will not do either," said the son of Na Kimanaueze.

"Do you wish to look for a bride among the people of a different country?" said Na Kimanaueze.

"No," said the son of Na Kimanaueze. "I do not want a bride from a different country."

"Who then will you marry?" said Na Kimanaueze.

"I will marry the daughter of the Sun and the Moon," said the son of Na Kimanaueze.

Na Kimanaueze did not know what to say at first. "You have great ambitions, my son, and I'm not sure they are realistic. How do you think you will be able to win that girl for a wife?"

"I don't know," said the son of Na Kimanaueze, "but I'm sure I'll find a solution some way."

Na Kimanaueze did not know what he could do to persuade his son to give up this silly idea, so he left his son to it, thinking that once he failed, he would come to his senses and marry a nice girl from their own village.

The son of Na Kimanaueze, for his part, thought and thought about how to go about asking for the hand of the daughter of the Sun and Moon. He decided that the best thing to do would be to write a letter asking her parents to let her be his bride. He thought very carefully about what to say, then wrote a respectful letter to the Sun and Moon and sealed it.

"Now to get it up to Heaven," said the son of Na Kimanaueze, and so he walked out of the village to see whether he could find someone to act as his messenger. The son of Na Kimanaueze came across a deer. "Hello, Deer," said the son of Na Kimanaueze. "Can you take a message to the Sun and Moon for me, please?"

"Oh, my!" said Deer. "I can't do that at all."

Then the son of Na Kimanaueze went to Antelope and said, "Hello, Antelope. Can you take a message to the Sun and Moon for me, please?"

"No," said Antelope. "I don't even know how to do that."

The son of Na Kimanaueze continued on his journey until he came across a hawk. "Hello, Hawk," said the son of Na Kimanaueze. "Can you take a message to the Sun and Moon for me, please?"

"I can fly very high and very well," said Hawk, "but I don't think I could get up far enough to deliver your message.

Next the son of Na Kimanaueze spoke with Vulture, but Vulture had the same answer as all the other animals. "I can't do that," said Vulture. "I tried once, but I couldn't fly high enough."

The son of Na Kimanaueze was very discouraged. He had asked all the animals he met whether they could be his messenger, and every single one told him no. The son of Na Kimanaueze sat down on the banks of a river to rest. He was very sad and despaired that his letter would ever be delivered.

Frog saw the son of Na Kimanaueze sitting there. Frog went to the son of Na Kimanaueze and said, "Why are you so sad?"

"I am sad because I want to marry the daughter of the Sun and the Moon, but I have no way to deliver my letter to them asking for her hand. I asked Deer and Antelope and Hawk and Vulture to help me, and many other animals besides, but they all said no."

"Oh!" said Frog. "Never fear; I think I can help you."

The son of Na Kimanaueze scoffed. "Hawk and Vulture said they couldn't do it, and they fly in the sky all day. How could a frog possibly hope to get into Heaven and bring my letter to the Sun and the Moon?"

"It is true that I cannot fly," said Frog, "but I know where the servants of the Sun and the Moon go to fetch water. I am not a flying animal, but I am a water animal, and if you entrust your letter to me, I will see it delivered, on my honor."

The son of Na Kimanaueze handed the letter to Frog. "Very well, I will trust you. But if it turns out that you have been lying to me, things will go very badly for you."

"I understand," said Frog, and then he hopped away with the son of Na Kimanaueze's letter in his mouth.

Frog hopped all the way to the well where the servants of the Sun and the Moon came to draw water. He made sure that no one was watching and then slipped into the water. He found a good place to hide and settled in to wait. Not long afterward, the servants came to the well and began putting their jugs into the well to draw water. Frog waited until just the right moment, then hopped into one of the jugs before anyone could see him.

When the servants had filled all their jugs, they went back up into Heaven using the webs that Spider had spun for them, and put the jugs in their proper places. Frog waited until the sounds of footsteps and voices faded, then he crawled out of the jug. Frog looked about the room and noticed that a table stood in the very middle. He hopped onto the table, left the letter there, then hopped down and found a place to hide and wait.

Frog didn't have to wait long. The Sun came into the room, thinking to drink some water, and he saw the letter with his name and his wife's name on the outside. He thought it very odd that a letter to him should be in the room where the water was kept. The Sun called all the servants together. He showed them the letter and asked, "Where did this letter come from?" But none of the servants knew.

The Sun opened the letter and read it. The letter said, "I, Kimanaueze kia Tumb' a Ndala, son of the chief Na Kimanaueze, respectfully ask the hand of the daughter of the Sun and Moon in marriage."

The Sun was very surprised. Why would a mortal man want to marry his daughter, and more importantly, how had a mortal man managed to deliver the letter all the way to Heaven without the Sun knowing about it? Then the Sun left the room, not saying anything to anyone about what was in the letter.

When Frog saw that it was safe, he jumped back into one of the jugs. When it was time to refill the jugs, the servants went down Spider's web and took all the jugs to the well, including the one Frog was in. The servants lowered the jugs into the water, and Frog jumped out without anyone seeing him.

Frog then went to the son of Na Kimanaueze and said, "I did it! I delivered your message to the Sun. He has read it, but I don't know what his reply will be."

"You are lying!" said the son of Na Kimanaueze. "You lie to me. You just hid that letter somewhere, and now you are pretending you went up to Heaven. Things will go very badly for you now."

"Wait!" said Frog. "Please trust me. Wait a while, and see whether the Sun answers you."

Six days passed with no answer from the Sun and the Moon. The son of Na Kimanaueze wrote another letter that said, "I, Kimanaueze kia Tumb' a Ndala, son of the chief Kimanaueze, wrote to you asking for your daughter's hand in marriage. It has been six days now, and I have received neither a yes nor a no from you." The son of Na Kimanaueze gave the letter to Frog and said, "Take this new letter up to Heaven, and see to it that you return with an answer this time."

Frog took the letter in his mouth and hopped over to the well. He hid in the well, and when the servants of the Sun and Moon came to get water, Frog jumped into one of the jugs. He waited until the servants had gone back up to Heaven on Spider's web, the jug had been put in its place, and the water room was empty before he jumped out and put the letter on the table. That done, he went to his hiding place.

Again the Sun came into the room to get a drink, and again he saw a letter on the table. The Sun asked the servants, "Has someone been giving you letters to bring to me?" But the servants all said no.

The Sun then wrote a reply to the son of Na Kimanaueze. The reply said, "I consent to let you marry my daughter on one condition: you must come to Heaven in person with your first bride-gift. I wish to meet you and know what kind of a man my daughter will be marrying." The Sun left the letter on the table and went out of the room.

When Frog thought it was safe, he came out of his hiding place and jumped up on the table. He picked up the Sun's letter and went to hide in one of the water jugs. In the morning, the servants picked up the jugs to refill them at the well, and Frog jumped out when his jug was lowered into the water. Then he went in search of the son of Na Kimanaueze to bring him the Sun's reply.

Frog went to the son of Na Kimanaueze's house with the letter and knocked on the door. From inside, the son of Na Kimanaueze said, "Who is there?"

"It is Frog, and I bring you the Sun's reply."

The son of Na Kimanaueze opened the door and saw Frog sitting there in front of the door, with a letter in his mouth. The son of Na Kimanaueze took the letter, and Frog hopped away to do his own business.

The son of Na Kimanaueze read the letter. He went to his chest and took out forty gold pieces. He put the gold into a bag and wrote another letter to the Sun. The letter said, "Here are forty gold pieces for the first gift. I have brought them as you asked. I wait to hear what you would consider a fair bride-price."

In the morning, the son of Na Kimanaueze went to the river. There he found Frog and said to him, "Please take this bag of money and this letter to Heaven."

Frog hopped away with the money and the letter. He went to the well and waited for the servants to take him up to Heaven in one of the jugs. When the water room was empty, Frog left the money and the letter on the table, then hid himself and waited.

The Sun came into the room and saw the bag and the letter on the table. He opened the bag and read the letter. He smiled and then went to show his wife, the Moon, what the son of Na Kimanaueze had sent.

"See, my wife? This suitor sends us a fine first present, and he is a chief's son to boot. I think he will make a fine husband for our daughter."

"Oh, yes," said the Moon. "I think we should let him marry her. I think we should make him a meal to eat while he is here."

The Moon called the servants and told them, "Roast a hen, and make other good things to eat. Then leave the platter on the table in the water room." When the meal was cooked, the servants took it and put it on the table, then they left. Frog came out of his hiding place and ate the meal, then went back to hide once more.

After a time, the Sun came back into the room and saw that the meal had been eaten. He wrote another letter and left it on the table. The letter said, "You have brought a fine first gift. My wife and I are pleased. Your bride-price shall be a large sack of gold coins."

Frog picked up the letter once it was safe and hopped back into one of the jugs. When he arrived back on Earth, he went to the son of Na Kimanaueze, gave him the Sun's reply, then went back to tend to his own business at the river.

The son of Na Kimanaueze read the letter and was very pleased to see the Sun's reply. He gathered up coins and put them into a large sack. Then he wrote a letter that said, "Here is the bride-price you requested. Soon I will write to you again to set the day for your daughter to become my bride."

In the morning, the son of Na Kimanaueze gave the letter and the sack of gold to Frog to take up to Heaven. Frog went up in one of the jugs, waited until the water room was empty, then left the gold and the letter on the table. He hopped over to his hiding place to wait, and soon thereafter the Sun and the Moon came to see what their daughter's suitor had left them. They saw the large sack of gold and read the son of Na Kimanaueze's letter, and they were both very pleased indeed. The Moon called her servants and told them, "Roast a young pig for our new son-in-law, and leave it here on the table."

The servants killed and roasted the pig. They put it on a platter and left it in the water room, then they went away. Frog jumped up on the table and ate all of the pig. Then he jumped back into one of the jugs and waited to be taken back down to Earth, where he jumped back into the well and waited for the servants to be gone.

Frog hopped away to the son of Na Kimanaueze's house. He knocked on the door, and when the son of Na Kimanaueze opened it, Frog said, "They have accepted your bride-price. Now you have to set the date for your wedding."

Now the son of Na Kimanaueze had a new problem. He couldn't send Frog up to Heaven to bring his bride down; surely Frog was too small for such a burden. But how to fetch the daughter of the Sun and the Moon down to Earth? The son of Na Kimanaueze went and asked all the large animals he could think of who might be able to go up to Heaven and bring his bride back down, but every animal said that they wouldn't be able to do that.

The son of Na Kimanaueze went back to the riverbank to sit and think. Frog saw him there and asked, "What is troubling you?"

"I cannot find anyone to bring my bride down from Heaven."

"Let me do that," said Frog.

"Oh, Frog, that is a very kind offer," said the son of Na Kimanaueze, "but surely you're too small for such a burden. Besides, I don't think I should ask you to do anything else for me; you've already helped me so very much, I hate to ask yet another thing from you."

"Never fear," said Frog. "I am very small, but I am also very clever, and I will bring your bride down to Earth for you."

"Thank you, my friend," said the son of Na Kimanaueze. "I will wait as patiently as I can for you to return with her."

Frog hopped away to the well to wait to be taken up to Heaven. When he arrived, he went to his favorite hiding place and waited until night fell. After many hours, the Sun went to bed, and everything was dark and quiet. Frog came out of his hiding place and hopped to the bedroom of the daughter of the Sun and Moon. He hopped onto the young woman's bed and took out her eyes. He wrapped the eyes securely in a clean cloth and then went back to his hiding place to sleep until morning.

Morning came. The Sun got up, and the servants began to go about their business. But there was something wrong; the daughter of the Sun and the Moon usually arose when her father did, but this morning she was nowhere to be found. A servant was sent to see whether she was well or not. The servant found her still in her bed, weeping.

"Why do you not get up?" said the servant.

"I do not get up because something is wrong with my eyes," said the young woman. "I cannot see."

The servant told the Sun and the Moon what was wrong with their daughter. They went to her chamber and asked, "What is wrong, my daughter?"

"Something is wrong with my eyes. I cannot see anything at all," she said.

The Sun called for messengers. When they arrived, the Sun said, "Go down to Earth. Find the witch doctor Ngombo. See whether he can tell us what is wrong with our daughter."

The messengers went to the house of Ngombo. When they arrived, they said, "We are here to ask your advice."

Ngombo went into his house and came back out with the things he needed to learn what needed to be done and why the messengers were there. Ngombo sat down upon the ground and cast his divining objects. He looked at them closely, then said, "You have come to ask me about someone who has an illness in their eyes. This person is a woman. Also, you were sent here to me; you did not come because you wanted to. Have I said true?"

"Yes," said the messengers. "Everything you said is true."

Then Ngombo cast his divining objects again. He looked at them closely, then said, "The woman who has an illness in her eyes is betrothed, but the wedding has not yet happened. Her husband-to-be says, 'I am the one that made the woman blind. Send her down to me. If you do not, she will die.' You must bring the woman to her husband as soon as may be. I have spoken my judgment. You must do as I have told you."

The messengers returned to Heaven and told the Sun everything that Ngombo had said. "Very well," said the Sun. "We will bring her down tomorrow."

In the morning, Frog returned to Earth in one of the water jugs. He went to the son of Na Kimanaueze's house and said, "You shall wed your bride this very day."

"I think you are lying, clever Frog," said the son of Na Kimanaueze. "I do not see her here."

"She will be here by sunset," said Frog. "Just you wait."

While Frog was returning to Earth in a jug, the Sun went to Spider and said, "I need to send my daughter down to her husband today. Can you weave a web strong enough to take her down safely?"

"Oh, yes," said Spider. "I will have it done before the end of the day."

Spider set to spinning a great web. She spun and spun and spun her silk. It took her almost all day, but finally it was ready.

Toward the end of the day, Frog went back to the well to wait. As the sun was starting to set, the Sun's servants took his daughter to Earth on the special web Spider had made for her. They brought her to the well where they fetched their water, then went back up to Heaven.

When Frog saw that the young woman was standing next to the well, he said, "Never fear! I am here to take you to your husband and to heal your eyes."

Frog gave the young woman back her eyes, then led her to the son of Na Kimanaueze's house. Frog knocked on the door, and when the son of Na Kimanaueze answered, Frog said, "Here indeed is your bride, the daughter of the Sun and the Moon."

The two young people looked upon each other and were very pleased. Soon the wedding was held, with much celebration, and the son of Na Kimanaueze and the daughter of the Sun and the Moon lived a long and happy life together.

Part II: Hero Tales

The Twin Brothers *(Cabinda Province, Angola)*

Cabinda is a province of Angola that sits outside the boundaries of that country. Cabinda is bordered instead by the Democratic Republic of the Congo to the south and east and by the Republic of the Congo to the north.

The story of the twin brothers told here is typical of the hero tale. We have two brothers, Mavungu and Lembe, who display remarkable growth and who have extraordinary powers. Here the powers are contained in a charm or fetish with which each boy is born and with which they can work all kinds of magic.

The story retold below follows a common arc: one brother heads off to seek his fortune, and when he does not return, the other goes looking for him. The search is successful, but unlike many other stories of this type, it does not end well; this story concludes with a violent twist.

Once there was a woman who was with child. When her time came to be delivered, her labor was very long and very difficult, but in the end she gave birth to two twin boys. The woman named the boys Mavungu and Lembe. Mavungu was the first to be born, and Lembe followed after.

Now, these boys were no ordinary children. They each were born with a valuable charm, and they each were nearly fully grown at birth. And so it was that Mavungu decided soon after he was born that he would set out on his travels.

At that time, the daughter of Nzambi, the creator of all things, was of an age to be married. The leopard went to Nzambi and said, "I would like the hand of your daughter in marriage."

Nzambi replied, "You will have to ask her consent first. It is up to her to decide who she will have for a husband."

The leopard went to Nzambi's daughter and asked her to marry him. She refused, and so the leopard went home, feeling very sad indeed.

Other animals came to offer themselves as husbands for Nzambi's daughter: the gazelle, the wild boar, and every other animal that had breath. One by one they asked for the young woman's hand, and one by one she refused them.

Mavungu soon learned that the daughter of Nzambi was receiving suitors. He decided that he would win her for his wife. Mavungu took his charm and asked it to help him in his quest. Then he took up many blades of grass, and with the help of the charm, he transformed them into different things that he could use on his journey. One blade of grass became a knife; another became a horse. In this way he transformed all the blades of grass until he felt he had everything he needed, and when this was done, he set out on his journey.

Mavungu traveled on and on. He went many, many miles, traveling all through the morning and well into the afternoon, until finally he became faint from hunger. He took out his charm and said to it, "Are you planning to let me starve?" In the blink of an eye, the charm set a delicious feast out for Mavungu. Mavungu ate and was happy and satisfied.

When he was done, Mavungu said, "O charm, it is not right that all these dishes should be left here on the ground for any passerby to take. Make them disappear." And so the charm made everything disappear.

Mavungu resumed his journey. Soon the sun began to set. Mavungu said to his charm, "I will need a place to sleep for the night," and so the charm prepared a good sleeping place for Mavungu where he could rest in comfort and safety until the morning.

When the sun rose, Mavungu told the charm to clear away his sleeping place and then resumed his journey. He journeyed on and on for many days, and for many more days after that, until finally he came to Nzambi's town. Nzambi's daughter happened to catch sight of him approaching, and she immediately fell in love with him. She ran to her father and mother and said, "I have seen the man who I will marry. I love him, and if I cannot marry him, my life will be over."

Mavungu made his way through the town and finally arrived at Nzambi's house, and there he spoke to Nzambi. "I have heard that your daughter is to be married," said Mavungu. "I offer myself to be her husband."

"Go and speak to her," said Nzambi. "If she consents, then you may marry her."

Mavungu went to speak to Nzambi's daughter, and when they first set eyes upon one another, they realized they loved one another. They embraced and then ran to tell the young woman's parents that they would like to be wed. And so it was that Mavungu and his bride were taken to a beautiful house, where they slept together while all the rest of the town danced and sang and feasted far into the night.

In the morning, Mavungu woke and noticed that the house contained a great many mirrors, every single one of which was covered by a cloth. Mavungu woke his bride and said, "Why are all these mirrors covered? I would like to see myself in one of them. Can you uncover it?"

"Certainly," said the young woman. She lifted the cloth of one of the mirrors, but when Mavungu looked into it, he saw not himself but the town in which he was born.

"Show me another," said Mavungu, and so the young woman unveiled that mirror too. In that mirror, Mavungu saw another town that he knew. The young woman unveiled mirror after mirror, and in each one Mavungu saw a place that he had been before.

Finally, there remained but one veiled mirror. "Unveil that one, too," said Mavungu.

"I dare not," said his bride.

"Why?" said Mavungu.

"Because that is a town from which no one has ever yet returned. If you but catch a glimpse of it, I know you will want to go there, and if you go, you will never come home to me."

"Even so, I wish to see it," said Mavungu.

The young woman refused even more strongly, but Mavungu kept asking her until finally she relented. When the veil was lifted from the mirror, Mavungu looked into it and saw a very horrible place that surely was the most dangerous town in the whole world.

Mavungu said, "That is a place I must go."

"No! Please don't go there!" said the young woman. "You will never come back to me, and I cannot live without you!"

But no matter how the young woman pleaded, and no matter how many tears she shed, Mavungu was steadfast in his resolve. He gathered up his things, mounted his horse, and set out in search of the horrible town from which no one had ever returned.

After many days on the road, Mavungu finally came to the outskirts of the town. There he saw an old woman sitting next to a fire.

"Greetings, Mother," said Mavungu. "May I have a bit of your fire to light my pipe?"

"Certainly," said the old woman. "Tie up your horse tightly, then come closer and take some for yourself."

Mavungu dismounted, tied up his horse tightly, then walked over to where the old woman was sitting. But when he had come near enough, the old woman killed him, and then she killed his horse.

Now, back in Mavungu's hometown, his twin brother, Lembe, became concerned, because he had not heard from Mavungu for a terribly long time. Lembe took his charm and a handful of grass, and using his charm, he transformed the grass into all the things he would need on his journey. One blade of grass became a knife, another became a horse, and so on until he had all the things he would need. Then Lembe set out in search of his brother.

After many days' travel, Lembe finally arrived at Nzambi's town. Nzambi caught sight of him and ran out to greet him. "Mavungu!" said Nzambi. "You've come home at last!"

"I am not Mavungu," said Lembe. "I am his brother, Lembe."

"Nonsense," said Nzambi. "I know who you are. You are my son-in-law, and now that you are home, we shall have a great feast!"

And so the feast was prepared, and everyone in the village rejoiced, especially Nzambi's daughter. She was so happy she could not stop dancing and singing, and she kept calling Lembe by his brother's name. No matter how often or how strongly Lembe protested, the young woman refused to believe that Lembe was not her husband.

When the sun set and the feast was over, Nzambi's daughter led Lembe to the house she shared with her husband. Lembe refused Nzambi's embraces, saying, "I am too tired from my journey. Perhaps another time." Nzambi's daughter was disappointed, but she did not protest. When she was fast asleep, Lembe told his charm to prepare a separate chamber for the young woman. The charm did as Lembe bid, and so Nzambi's daughter slept in one place and Lembe slept in another. In the morning, the charm let Nzambi's daughter out, so she did not know that she had not slept with Lembe.

In the morning, Lembe noticed that the house was all full of mirrors covered with cloths. As his brother had done before him, Lembe asked Nzambi's daughter to remove the veils and let him see the mirrors. She removed the veils one by one until the only one left was the mirror that showed the terrible town. Nzambi's daughter refused at first to remove the veil from that mirror, but finally she gave in to Lembe's insistence and let him see it. As soon as Lembe looked into the mirror, he knew where his brother had gone.

Lembe prepared to go and find his brother, but when Nzambi found out what he was doing, he said, "Please don't leave. That is a terrible place you are going to. Nobody ever comes back alive. Think of my daughter, your young wife. You are barely married, and the whole time you were gone, she pined and grieved."

Lembe said, "Yes, I know, and I am sorry for her distress, but I must go on this journey. And you needn't fear: I already came back from there once, so surely I shall come back a second time."

And so Lembe set out on his journey, and after many days' travel, he came to the outskirts of the town. There he saw the old woman sitting next to her fire. "Greetings, Mother," said Lembe. "May I have a bit of your fire with which to light my pipe?"

"Certainly," said the old woman. "Tie your horse up tightly, then come and get some for yourself."

Lembe dismounted, but when he tied up his horse, he only did so loosely. Then he headed over to the fire, and when he got to where the old woman was sitting, he killed her. When the old woman was dead, Lembe looked for his brother's bones and the bones of his horse. Soon enough, he found them, and when he had put them all in order, he touched them with his charm. Mavungu and his horse came back to life again.

Mavungu and Lembe rejoiced to see one another again, and when they were done greeting one another, they looked for the bones of all the people the old woman had killed and brought them back to life. Then they set off on the journey back to Nzambi's town, with all the resurrected people following them.

On the way back to Nzambi's town, Lembe explained what had happened while he was there, how everyone kept insisting that he was Mavungu, and how Lembe had made sure that he and his brother's wife had slept separately. Mavungu was very grateful that his brother had been so thoughtful.

They journeyed on for a little while, then Lembe said, "What shall we do about all our followers?"

"I think I should be their leader because I am the eldest," said Mavungu.

"Yes, but it was I who brought you back to life," said Lembe. "Surely that counts for something."

The brothers argued and argued, and finally Mavungu became so angry that he killed his brother. Mavungu and his followers resumed their journey, but Lembe's horse stayed behind with Lembe's body. When the others were well out of sight, the horse took Lembe's charm and touched it to his body. Lembe came back to life again. Then he mounted his horse and went in search of his brother.

Meanwhile, Mavungu arrived home with all his followers. Nzambi and the rest of the town rejoiced greatly to see that he had returned safely, but none rejoiced more than Mavungu's wife. As before, Nzambi commanded a great feast be held to celebrate Mavungu's safe return.

In the middle of the festivities, Lembe arrived. He went up to Mavungu and killed him. The townspeople were horrified, but Lembe explained what had happened, and the people agreed that Lembe had acted correctly.

The Tale of Uthlakanyana *(Zulu, South Africa)*

Uthlakanyana is the trickster hero of a series of Zulu tales, two of which are retold below. Like many tricksters and heroes, Uthlakanyana has a miraculous origin and exhibits superhuman powers starting from the day he is born. He begins showing his tricksterish side right at the beginning, first fooling all of the men of the village by tricking them out of their meat, then by fooling his mother by eating the birds she had cooked while she was still asleep, then convincing her that she had cooked them so long only the heads were left. The second story also revolves around cooking and food, but this time the victims of Uthlakanyana's cleverness is a family of cannibals. Uthlakanyana tricks the cannibal mother into getting herself boiled to death and then tricks her sons into eating her.

To Western readers, Uthlakanyana's treatment of his own mother might seem odd at best and callous at worst, but in a note to his retelling of the tale, author Henry Callaway says that this likely is an attempt on Uthlakanyana's part to give himself a reasonable excuse for leaving, without which he cannot cut ties with his mother to go out into the world by himself.

The Birth of Uthlakanyana

There once was a woman who was expecting a child. When the time grew near for her to be delivered, she heard a small voice say, "Mother! Give birth to me now! The people are eating all of my father's cattle!"

"What is this?" thought the mother. "It is not time for my child to be born, and an infant cannot speak. I must be hearing things."

But again the voice came, saying, "Mother! Give birth to me now! The people are eating all of my father's cattle!"

The woman went to her husband, who was the king of the village and who was in the kraal slaughtering some cattle. The woman told her husband what had happened. The people there also heard what the woman said. "Let us hear what the child says!" said the people.

"Yes!" said the father. "Let us all be silent so that we might hear the child together."

Everyone held very still and waited. Soon the voice came from the mother's womb, saying, "Mother! Give birth to me now! The people are eating all of my father's cattle, and I have not yet had my share!"

All the people agreed that this was a very wondrous thing. Then the father said, "All of you should go to your own homes. My wife will go into our home and give birth now."

Everyone left the house, and the woman gave birth to the child. When the woman saw her child, she was quite astonished, for although he was very small, he looked like an old man and could already stand and walk by himself. The child went to the place where the men were sitting around a fire eating meat. When the men saw the creature approach, they became afraid and ran away, for the creature was small like an infant but looked like an old man. The child paid the men no heed. He simply took a piece of meat that the men had cooked, then sat down by the fire and began to eat.

The men then went to the mother of the child and said, "That creature there eating meat by our fire: is that the child who spoke within you and to whom you have just given birth?"

"Yes, indeed it is," said the mother.

The men marveled at this. "This is a wonder that has been wrought for us. Surely you are a queen, and this child is to be a great one among us."

The child heard what the men and his mother said about him, so he went to his father and said, "Father, I know that you and the others think that I am but a child, but I am not. I wish you to hold a test that will prove that I am a man full grown. Gather all the men and boys of the village into the kraal. Then take the whole haunch of an ox, and throw it outside the kraal. At your word, all the men and boys will try to be the first to get the haunch and take it back into the kraal. Whoever does this will be known as a man for certain."

The father agreed that it was well to do this, so he gathered all the men and boys into the kraal. Then he took the haunch of an ox and threw it outside the kraal. At the father's word, all the men and boys surged toward the gate of the kraal, pushing and shoving each other, trying to be the first to go through the gate and thus be the first to seize the haunch. But the child stayed away from the mass of bodies and instead crawled beneath the bars of the kraal. He ran over to the haunch, picked it up, raised it over his head, and then brought it to his mother to cook before the first of the men and boys finally managed to escape through the gate.

When the child arrived at his mother's house with the ox's haunch, he said to her, "Mother, here is the meat I have brought you."

His mother replied, "This is a good day, and I am very happy because my child is a very wise man."

The child then went back to the kraal, where his father was butchering a steer and giving meat to the men of the village. The father was about to give a piece of meat to one of the men when the child walked up and said, "Give me that meat. I shall put it in your house for you."

"Certainly," said the man.

"Thank you," said the child.

The child took the meat and went into the man's house. He took some of the blood from the meat and smeared it onto the storage mat and hanging stick, then brought the meat to his mother's house. When that was done, the child returned to the kraal, where his father was about to give a piece of meat to another man.

"Give me that meat," said the child. "I shall put it in your house for you."

"Certainly," said the man.

"Thank you," said the child.

As he had done with the first man's portion, the child took the meat and smeared some blood on the man's storage mat and hanging stick, but then brought the meat to his own mother's house. In this way, the child took the meat meant for each man of the village but brought it to his own mother instead.

When the men went into their houses, they saw that the storage mats and hanging sticks all had blood on them but that the meat was nowhere to be found, for every last piece had been taken to the house of the child's mother. The men went to the child and said, "We gave you our meat, and you said you would put it in our houses. There is blood on the storage mat as though it had been laid there and on the hanging stick as though it had been used to hang the meat, but we cannot find the meat anywhere. What have you done with our meat?" But the child would give them no answer other than that the meat was in their houses and that the blood on the utensils testified to that.

The women of the village had watched what had happened all day. When they saw the confusion of their men, they all said, "Do you not understand? This child is Uthlakanyana. Have you not seen that although he has the stature of a child, he walks and talks and behaves like a man? Have you not understood that he has tricked you well today, not once, but many times? Surely he was not begotten in the usual way. Surely the king of our village is not his father. This child is different and wondrous. He spoke while he was yet in the womb, and he has bested every man in this village on the very day he was but newly born. He will surely do many great things."

Uthlakanyana and the Cannibal

One day, Uthlakanyana went down to the river to hunt. While he was looking for prey, he came across a great many bird traps. Each one of them had a bird in it. Some traps even had two or three! Uthlakanyana took all the birds from the traps and brought them home to his mother.

"Mother, please take this heavy load from me," he said.

"What load is it you carry, my son?" said his mother.

"I caught a great many birds when I went out hunting today, and I am weary from carrying them all."

The mother took the birds from her son and marveled at how many he had caught. "My son is a man full grown, and a wise one, too!" she said. "Look at this fine catch of birds he brings to me!"

"Cook all of them, Mother," said the child. "Put them in a pot, and seal it well with cow dung. Set it over the fire overnight, and I will eat them in the morning. But for tonight, I shall be sleeping elsewhere. I shall go to the house where all the other boys sleep." And with that, the child went out of his mother's house and went to the house where all the boys slept together.

When the child arrived at the house where the boys were sleeping, they all said to him, "Get out! We don't want you here."

"Why?" said the child. "I am a boy and so should be allowed to sleep here with you, who are all boys yourselves. What, do you think I am a girl?"

"No," said the boys, "but we do not trust you. You took all the meat that belonged to our fathers, the meat that the king had given them. And we know that the king is not really your father."

"Is that so?" said the child. "Who is my father, then?"

"Oh, we have no idea," the boys replied, "but you are some kind of wonder-child, that is for sure, and likely will get up to some kind of mischief if we let you sleep here."

"All right, then," said the child, "I was thinking of leaving, but since you're making a fight out of this, I will stay and sleep here just to spite you."

The boys scoffed. "You couldn't fight us if you tried. You might be very clever with words, but you were just born yesterday, and you don't have the strength to best us. But you are very clever with words, and neither we nor our fathers can best you in that way." And then the boys turned their backs to the child and went to sleep. Soon Uthlakanyana went to sleep, too.

In the morning, Uthlakanyana went back to his mother's house. There he found his mother was still sleeping. Uthlakanyana unsealed the pot where the birds were cooking and found that they were ready to eat. He ate the bodies but left the heads behind. Then he went outside and got some cow dung. He put it in the bottom of the pot and placed the bird heads on top of it. After he did this, he sealed the pot up again, just like it had been before he ate the birds, and during all of this, his mother slept on.

Uthlakanyana left his mother's house. He walked a little way into the village, then turned around and went back. He stopped outside the door to his mother's house and said, "Mother! I am here! Open the door, please!" His mother opened the door for him, and he went into her house.

"Oh, I am so very hungry, and it's already so late in the morning," said Uthlakanyana. "Surely you have slept too much. Those birds have probably turned all to dung inside the pot for having been left there so long."

Uthlakanyana unsealed the pot and opened the lid. "Look! I was right! They're all turned to dung."

"How did this happen?" said his mother.

"I know how it happened, even if you don't," said Uthlakanyana. "I am a grown man, but you are a small child. I spoke to you when I was yet in the womb, telling you to give birth to me. I am older than you, so very, very old. And you are not my mother, and your husband, the king, is not my father. It pleased me to be born from you, but now it is time for me to leave. I must go traveling all about, but you and your husband must stay here and live together."

The mother took the bird heads and the cow dung out of the pot. "Truly you spoke when you said the bodies would be turned to dung," she said.

"Let me see them," said Uthlakanyana, and when she showed the bird heads to him, he took them and ate them all. Then he said to his mother, "You ate up all my birds, so I have eaten all the heads." Then Uthlakanyana took up his staff and left his mother's house and started off on his travels, muttering the whole time about how angry he was that his mother had eaten all the birds herself and left him nothing but the heads.

Uthlakanyana walked and walked, and then he came upon a place where many bird traps had been set. The traps each had birds in them, and so Uthlakanyana took them, thinking that they would make a fine meal later on. But the traps belonged to a wicked cannibal, and no sooner had Uthlakanyana removed the last bird from the traps than the cannibal grabbed him and shouted, "Why are you taking my birds from my traps?"

"Oh, please, please don't hurt me," said Uthlakanyana, dropping all the birds. "I didn't take anything! Please let me go!"

But the cannibal was very clever; he had smeared the traps with birdlime, and Uthlakanyana had some of it on his hands. "You did indeed take my birds," said the cannibal, "for I see your hands are smeared with the birdlime I put on the traps to catch thieves such as yourself."

"Please let me go!" said Uthlakanyana. "Please don't hurt me. Take me home to your mother. On the way we can clean off the birdlime, and if you treat me well, I will cook up nicely. Take me home to your mother, and she can cook me for your dinner. But you must leave the house while I am cooking because otherwise the dish will spoil and will not be worth eating."

"Very well," said the cannibal, and so he picked up the birds Uthlakanyana had dropped and took him to his mother's house. When they arrived, the cannibal said to his mother, "Look at this little thief I caught stealing from my traps. He says that he will cook up nicely but that I need to leave the house while he is in the pot. It's already late in the day, and I am tired. Cook him tomorrow morning after I have left the house." Then the cannibal and his mother gave Uthlakanyana a place to sleep, and they went to their own beds.

In the morning, the cannibal said to his mother, "Mother, cook up my little thief. Cook him well so that I will have a tasty dinner when I come home." Then the cannibal went out.

Uthlakanyana said to the cannibal's mother, "I will be more tender and tastier if you put me on the roof to dry out a bit in the sun before you cook me. You can go back to bed until I'm well dried. I'll call you when I'm done."

"Very well," said the cannibal's mother, and so she put Uthlakanyana on the roof of the house and went back to bed.

Now, this was a very clever thing Uthlakanyana had done, for from the roof of the house he could see which way the cannibal had gone. The cannibal walked a little way away from the house, where he met his brother, and together they walked away and went over the rise of a hill.

When the cannibal and his brother were gone, Uthlakanyana came down from the roof and went into the house. "I'm all dried," he said. "Let's start cooking. I know a game that we can play that will make me into the tastiest dish your son has ever eaten. I will show you how to play. We will need the biggest pot you have, for when I am all boiled, I shall swell up, and we don't want the pot to boil over."

The mother got her biggest pot, filled it with water, then set it over the fire. When that was done, Uthlakanyana said, "Here is how we play. First, I boil myself a little bit, then I get out of the pot. Then you climb in and boil yourself a little bit. Then we trade places."

After waiting for the water to warm a bit, Uthlakanyana took the lid off the pot and tested the water with his hand. "Oh, yes," he said, "that is hot enough to start cooking me."

The cannibal's mother took Uthlakanyana and put him in the pot, then sealed the pot with a lid. After a little while, Uthlakanyana said, "It's time for your turn! Take me out, please."

When Uthlakanyana was out of the pot, he looked at the fire. "Oh, dear. That will never do. We must build up the fire a bit." And so he built up the fire until it was roaring well under the pot, and the water was beginning to steam and bubble. "Look!" he said, "That means it's ready for you. Take off all your clothes and get in. It's quite warm and lovely in there."

When the cannibal's mother was undressed, Uthlakanyana put her in the pot and covered it with a lid. Soon the mother began to cry out from inside the pot. "Oh, help! Let me out! I am boiled to death! Let me out!"

"How can you say you are already boiled to death?" said Uthlakanyana. "If you were dead, you wouldn't be able to talk. No, I don't believe you. You must finish your turn in the pot, just as I finished mine."

After a little while, Uthlakanyana said to the mother, "Hey, there! Are you boiled yet?" But there was no reply from the pot, so Uthlakanyana said, "Ah, she must be well boiled now, because she doesn't answer me."

Then Uthlakanyana put on the cannibal's mother's clothes, and his body grew until it fit the garments perfectly. He lay down on the mother's bed and waited for her son to come home. Soon enough, the cannibal and his brother returned. "Hello, Mother," the cannibal said. "Is that little thief cooked nicely and ready to eat?"

"Oh, yes," said Uthlakanyana, pretending to be the cannibal's mother. "He cooked up very nicely. He even expanded quite a bit in the pot, so there's even more meat there than I thought there would be. You and your brother help yourselves; I've already eaten my share, and it was very good indeed."

The cannibals opened the pot and took out an arm. "Wait," said the cannibal's brother. "This looks an awful lot like Mother's arm."

"You shouldn't say that," said the cannibal. "You're going to bring a curse down upon Mother."

"I'm sorry," said the brother. "I take it back."

And so they ate the arm.

When the arm was gone, they reached into the pot and took out a leg. The cannibal's brother looked at the foot and said, "Doesn't this look an awful lot like Mother's foot? But I suppose I shouldn't say that, since I don't want to bring down a curse upon her."

Pretending to be the cannibals' mother, Uthlakanyana said, "Please don't worry; I'm over here, safe and sound. It's just the little thief who is in the pot." Then he got up and went to the door of the house. "I'm going out for a little while," he said. "You two boys finish your dinner. There's plenty there!"

The cannibal reached into the pot and drew out the other leg. He looked very closely at the foot and said, "Wait. This looks an awful lot like Mother's foot."

Uthlakanyana, meanwhile, walked quickly away from the house, and when he came to a place where he thought the cannibals might not be able to see him, he took off the mother's clothing and ran as fast as he could. When he had run far enough that he knew the cannibals would never be able to catch up to him, he turned and shouted, "Hey, cannibals! That was your mother's arm, and those were your mother's legs. You two fools have eaten your own mother!"

The cannibals heard Uthlakanyana and ran after him. "I told you that was our mother's hand and that was our mother's foot," said the brother as they ran. "I told you so, but you wouldn't listen."

Uthlakanyana ran until he came to the banks of a river. He knew the cannibals were chasing him, but the river was too deep to ford and too swift to swim, so he changed himself into a stick. Not long afterward, the cannibals arrived. "Now where has that little thief got to? said the cannibal.

"I think he must have crossed the river," said the brother. "See, here are his footprints on the bank."

The cannibal picked up the stick and threw it across the river in anger. But when the stick landed on the other side, it turned back into Uthlakanyana. "Thank you for throwing me across!" he said, and then ran away. The two cannibals stood on their side of the river, watching him go, and feeling very foolish indeed that they had been tricked that way. Then they went home, and Uthlakanyana continued on his own travels.

The Little Wise Woman *(Khoekhoe, South Africa)*

The Khoekhoe live in southwestern Africa and traditionally follow a nomadic pastoralist lifestyle. Formerly, these people were often referred to as "Hottentots," but that word has derogatory connotations. The term "Khoekhoe" used here refers to various Khoe-speaking peoples in Southern Africa.

The tale of the "little wise woman" retold below participates in the trope of the disadvantaged person who has special powers or insights that the advantaged people around them do not have. Both the little girl, who is the main protagonist, and the one-eyed man, who is the main antagonist, are disadvantaged in some way, the little girl by her age and size, and the one-eyed man by his half-blind state. Each of them uses their abilities to try to gain advantage, and each of them is ignored by the people around them who see them as lesser, to their own detriment. The only exception is the little girl's elder sister, who defends her younger sister and is willing to listen and follow instructions. In this way, she avoids the tragic fate of the other girls who treated the little wise woman dismissively.

The item of clothing called a kaross *mentioned in the story is made from animal hide with the wool or hair still attached. It is stitched together into a sleeveless jacket and is traditionally worn by the Khoekhoe people.*

A girl once set out to look for onions. She arrived at a place where she knew she could find some and found that a group of men had already arrived there before her. One of the men had only a single eye. The girl bent down to dig up the onions, and the men helped her. When her sack was full, the men said, "Why don't you go home and invite your friends to join you? There are plenty of onions for everyone."

The girl returned home and told all her friends about the onion field, but made no mention of the men. In the morning, the girls all picked up their sacks and set out to the onion field, with a little girl following after them.

"Why don't you tell your little sister to go home?" said one of the girls to the small one's elder sister. "She really shouldn't be coming with us."

"She's able to run by herself," said the elder sister. "It's not like any of us will need to carry her. Let her follow along."

When they arrived at the onion field, the little girl looked at the ground and saw there were many, many footprints. This made her uneasy. She went to the girl who had been there the day before and asked, "Why are there so many footprints? Weren't you alone last time?"

"Oh, those must be all mine," said the older girl. "I was walking around a lot, after all."

The little one didn't say anything else, keeping her suspicions to herself. She was a wise little woman and so kept looking about her while she worked. One time, she looked about and saw an anteater's hole.

The little one went back to digging onions, but kept looking up from time to time. She discovered that there were men close by, but she gave no sign that she had seen them, and the men seemingly could not see her.

When the little one had stopped working to look around yet again, one of the older girls said, "Why do you keep doing that? Just dig onions like the rest of us."

The little girl didn't reply, but she didn't stop looking either. After a little while, she stood up to look again, and she saw a group of men coming toward the field. One of them was the one-eyed man, and he was playing on a reed pipe. The little girl listened closely and discovered she could understand what the pipe was saying. Over and over, the reed pipe sang:

There will be blood, today blood will flow

There will be blood, today blood will flow

The girls heard the music of the reed pipe and began to dance. The little girl asked the older ones whether they could understand what the reed pipe was saying, but they all told her to stop asking silly questions. The little girl then started dancing with the others, but she made her way over to where her elder sister was dancing and tied her sister's *kaross* to her own, and they kept dancing together like that as the other girls became merrier and merrier. Soon the other girls were making so much noise and having so much fun that the two sisters thought they could slip away undetected.

As they walked away from the onion field, the little girl asked her sister, "Do you understand what the reed pipe is saying?"

"No, I don't," said the elder.

"It is saying, 'There will be blood, today blood will flow,' over and over."

Now, the little sister was truly a wise woman. She had her elder sister walk in front while she walked behind. The little girl stepped into her elder sister's footprints, which made it look like there was only one set of tracks, but she walked backward, so it wasn't possible to tell which direction they were going. The two girls walked like this until they came to the anteater's hole, where they climbed inside to hide.

After a little while, they heard the girls who were still in the field crying and screaming. The men had begun killing them, one after the other. The two sisters who had escaped heard the crying, and the elder one began to weep herself in grief for her friends. The little one said to her, "Be glad you came with me; if you had stayed, you would be dead just like all the others."

Back in the onion field, the men finished killing all the girls. The one-eyed man looked about and said, "Wait. There are two missing."

The other men said, "How would you even know that? You only have one eye."

"I do know," said the one-eyed man. "There are two others. We should go look for them."

The other men agreed to help look, and soon they found a single set of footprints outside the field. They couldn't decide whether these were the footprints of someone leaving or someone entering the field, but they decided to follow them out of the field anyway. Soon they came to the anteater's hole. They looked inside but didn't see anything. Then the one-eyed man looked. "They're in there!" he said.

The others laughed at him. "How would you even know that? You only have one eye."

"I do know," said the one-eyed man. "Look again, and you'll see them there."

The others looked again, but they still saw nothing, for the girls had hidden themselves behind a mass of cobwebs.

"I'll test whether there's really anyone in there," said one of the men. He took his assegai and thrust it into the hole. The tip of the assegai cut the elder sister's foot and it began to bleed, but before the man could pull the assegai out of the hole, the little sister wiped all the blood off. Then she said to her sister, "Don't cry or they will hear us."

When the assegai came back without any blood on it, the one-eyed man peered into the hole again. This time the little girl stared right back at him. The one-eyed man said to his companions, "I swear to you they are both inside that hole." But the other men jeered and said, "How would you even know that? You only have one eye."

The day had grown very hot, and the men became thirsty. They said to the one-eyed man, "We are going to get something to drink. You stay here and keep watch. You can get your drink when we come back."

The girls heard the other men leave, and when they were sure that the one-eyed man was alone, they began to sing a spell to him.

You dirty son of your father

Are you not thirsty as well?

You dirty son of your father

Dirty child of your father

Do you not also want to drink?

The one-eyed man fell under their spell. He said, "I'm too thirsty to wait for the others to come back," and then he left to get a drink for himself.

When the girls were sure the one-eyed man had gone, they crawled out of the hole. The little sister took her big sister on her back, and in this way they began to journey home. The way they had to go was across a plain that was flat and without trees, so when the men finished their drink and resumed looking for the girls, they saw them there in the distance. "There they go!" shouted the men, and they began to run after the girls.

The girls saw the men running toward them, so they turned themselves into thorn bushes. The beads the girls were wearing became drops of gum. The men arrived at the thorn bushes. They pulled the gum drops off the bushes and ate it. Then they lay down on the ground and went to sleep.

While the men were sleeping, the girls took the gum and smeared it on the eyes of the men, sealing them shut. Then the girls resumed their journey home.

When the girls had almost reached their kraal, the men woke up and found their eyes had been sealed shut with gum. "Oh, you layabouts!" said the one-eyed man. "You fell asleep and let the girls get away!"

"It's not like you're any better," said the men. "You fell asleep too, and your one eye is sealed shut just like our two eyes are."

The men removed the gum from their eyes and resumed looking for the girls, but they discovered that the girls had arrived safely at their parents' house, and so the men returned to their own village.

The girls told their parents what had happened and explained to the other villagers what had become of their daughters. The whole village wept and was in mourning but no one dared return to the onion field, not even to fetch the bodies of their daughters.

Part III: Cautionary Tales

The City Where People are Mended *(Hausa, Nigeria and Niger)*

The Hausa people are the most numerous of all African cultures, and the Hausa language is the most widely spoken, second only to Arabic. Primarily located in the Sahel and savannah regions of what are now Niger and Nigeria, Hausa communities are also found in neighboring states such as Cameroon, Chad, and Ghana, with others as far away as Eritrea. The Hausa people have embraced Islam since the Middle Ages, and many of their cities became important centers for trade along traditional African and Middle Eastern caravan routes.

The story retold below participates in several tropes common to folktales in many cultures. One such trope is the contrast between the good mother and the bad one, which goes hand in glove with the trope of the beautiful and ugly daughters. One twist on the latter, however, is that rather than being an antagonist in her own right—as she is in many other tales—the ugly daughter here is an innocent victim of her mother's own jealousy and greed. Jealousy and greed contrasted with generosity and mercy form the last trope, and also turn this story into a cautionary tale about treating others with respect.

The story mentions several types of food. One of these is fura, *balls of dough made of millet flour. The other is the fruit of the* adduwa *tree, which is similar to dates, although not as sweet.*

One day, the girls of the village decided to go into the forest to pick herbs. While they were in the forest, a great storm blew up from the east, sending down sheets and sheets of rain. The girls all ran to take shelter beneath a baobab tree, but when they found the tree was hollow, they went inside. No sooner had the girls entered the tree than the Devil came and closed it up behind them.

"Oh, please let us out!" cried the girls.

"No, I won't let you out," said the Devil, "not unless you give me your necklace and your clothes."

The girls handed the Devil their necklaces and clothes, except for one girl who refused. The ones who gave the Devil their things were let go, but the Devil kept the other one inside the tree. The girls who escaped ran to their friend's mother and told her everything that had happened and that the Devil still held the woman's daughter captive inside the baobab tree.

"Take me to the tree that I may know which one it is," said the mother. The girls led her to the tree, and the mother saw that there was a hole in the top that led down inside the trunk. The mother went home and cooked a meal for her daughter, then returned to the tree.

"Daughter!" she called. "I am here! I have food for you! Stretch your hand through the hole in the trunk, and I will give you your meal."

The girl heard her mother's voice, and so she put her hand through the hole in the trunk and received the food her mother had prepared. Once the girl had eaten all her food, the mother went home.

Now, there happened to be a hyena skulking nearby, and he saw and heard everything that went on. Thinking to take advantage of the situation, he went over to the tree and said, "Daughter! I am here! I have food for you! Stretch your hand through the hole in the trunk, and I will give you your meal."

The girl heard the hyena calling to her from outside the tree. She did not recognize the hyena's gruff voice. "You are not my mother," the girl said. "Go away."

The hyena went to a blacksmith's shop. "Change my voice so that I sound like a human," said the hyena.

"Very well," said the blacksmith, "but likely you'll eat the first thing you find in the road and that will undo all my work."

The blacksmith changed the hyena's voice, and the hyena trotted off on his way back to the tree. Along the road, the hyena came across a centipede. "Never pass up a free meal!" said the hyena, and he gobbled up the centipede in one bite.

Soon the hyena arrived at the baobab tree. "Daughter!" he called. "I am here! I have food for you! Stretch your hand through the hole in the trunk, and I will give you your meal."

But the hyena's voice was gruff and scratchy from having eaten the centipede, so the girl did not recognize it. "You are not my mother," the girl said. "Go away."

The hyena ran back to the blacksmith's shop in a fury. "You said you changed my voice, but it didn't work! I should gobble you up right where you stand!"

"Wait!" said the blacksmith. "Did you eat anything after I changed it the first time?"

"Well, yes," said the hyena. "There was a fat centipede in the road, and I was in the mood for a snack."

"That's why your voice changed back," said the blacksmith. "I'll fix it for you again; just don't eat me, and don't eat anything else yourself until after you've used the human voice."

The hyena went back to the baobab tree, this time taking care not to eat anything on the way. He arrived at the tree and called out, "Daughter! I am here! I have food for you! Stretch your hand through the hole in the trunk, and I will give you your meal."

This time the girl was fooled. She thought it was her mother calling to her, so she put her hand up through the hole in the tree. No sooner had she done this than the hyena jumped up and grabbed the girl's hand. He pulled the girl out of the tree and ate her on the spot, leaving only the bones behind, and then he went away.

When evening came, the girl's mother returned to the tree to give food to her daughter, and there she saw her daughter's bones lying on the ground. The mother wailed to find the dead body of her child. Then she went home to get a basket. She returned to the tree and tenderly collected all the bones. When she had every last bone, she set off to find the city where people were mended.

The mother traveled a long way down the road until she came to a place where food was cooking itself over a fire. "Food, can you tell me how to get to the city where people are mended?" asked the mother.

"Won't you eat me? Please, have a bite!" said the food.

"How can I eat when my daughter is dead? I will not eat you," said the mother.

"Very well," said the food. "Go down that road until you come to the place where it splits right and left. Take the right-hand road, and leave the one on the left behind."

The woman thanked the food and went down the road. On and on she walked until she came to a place where meat was roasting itself over a fire. "Meat, can you tell me how to get to the city where people are mended?" asked the mother.

"Won't you eat me? Please, have a bite!" said the meat.

"How can I eat when my daughter is dead? I will not eat you," said the mother.

"Very well," said the meat. "Go down that road until you come to the place where it splits right and left. Take the right-hand road, and leave the one on the left behind."

Again the woman walked down the road until she came to a pot where *fura* was being mixed. "*Fura*, can you tell me how to get to the city where people are mended?" asked the mother.

"Won't you eat me? Please, have a bite!" said the *fura*.

"How can I eat when my daughter is dead? I will not eat you," said the mother.

"Very well," said the *fura*. "Go down that road until you come to the place where it splits right and left. Take the right-hand road, and leave the one on the left behind."

The woman continued her journey, following the directions she had been given, and soon she arrived at the city where people were mended. She entered the city, and the people asked, "Why are you here?"

"I am here because the hyena ate my daughter, and I wish her to be mended," said the woman.

"Do you have all her bones?" asked the people.

"Yes, they are here in this basket."

"We will mend your daughter tomorrow," said the people.

The people gave the woman a place to sleep, and in the morning, they said, "Please go out and tend our cattle."

The woman went to the byre and let the cattle out into the pasture. Now, the food of these cattle was the fruit of the *adduwa* tree. The woman went to the tree and picked off all the ripe fruit and fed it to the cattle. Then she took some of the unripe fruit for herself and ate it. The woman fed the cattle ripe *adduwa* fruit all day, and at sunset, she brought them home and put them in their byre. No sooner had they reached the byre than the biggest bull started singing,

This woman is a good woman

She fed us ripe fruit all day

And kept none for herself

This woman is a good woman

Mend her daughter well!

The people heard the bull's song. They said to the woman, "Go into that hut and sleep well. Your daughter will be given back to you in the morning."

Sure enough, when the woman awoke in the morning, the people gave her her daughter back. The mother and daughter greeted one another with great joy, and then they went home together.

Now, the mother was not the only wife in that household. There was another wife, who was jealous because her daughter was ugly whereas the first wife's daughter was beautiful. The second wife saw the first one return with her beautiful daughter restored, and when the second wife had heard the tale of what happened, she began to scheme about how she might get her daughter restored as well. Maybe she might even become beautiful afterward!

The second wife called her daughter to her, and threw her into a large mortar. Then the second wife began to pound her daughter with the pestle. "No, mother! Do not kill me!" pleaded her daughter. But the second wife did not stop. She pounded her daughter until she was dead, and then she collected all the bones in a basket and set out for the city where people were mended.

The second wife traveled a long way along the road until she came to the place where food was cooking itself. "Food, can you tell me how to get to the city where people are mended?" said the second wife.

"Won't you eat me? Please, have a bite!" said the food.

The second wife looked at the good food and said, "You don't have to ask twice," and then she ate up all the food.

When the food was all gone, the second wife resumed her journey. On and on she walked until she came to the place where meat was roasting itself. "Meat, can you tell me how to get to the city where people are mended?" said the second wife.

"Won't you eat me? Please, have a bite!" said the meat.

The second wife looked at the good meat and said, "You don't have to ask twice," and then she ate up all the meat.

Again the second wife walked down the road until she came to a pot where *fura* was being mixed. "*Fura*, can you tell me how to get to the city where people are mended?" asked the mother.

"Won't you eat me? Please, have a bite!" said the *fura*.

The second wife looked at the good *fura* and said, "You don't have to ask twice," and then she ate up all the *fura*.

Once all the fura was gone, the second wife resumed her journey. After much walking, she arrived at the city where people were mended. The people of the city saw the second wife enter with her basket and asked, "Why are you here?"

The second wife said, "Oh, it is a very sad tale. A hyena ate my daughter, and I have brought her here to be mended."

"Do you have all the bones?" said the people.

"I do; they are in this basket."

The people took the basket and said, "We will mend your daughter tomorrow." Then they showed the second wife to a place where she could sleep for the night.

In the morning, the people told the second wife, "Please look after our cattle today."

"Very well," said the second wife, and she let the cattle out of their byre and took them out into the pasture. When the second wife got to the orchard of *adduwa* trees, she picked all the green fruit and gave it to the cattle while eating all the ripe fruit herself. The second wife fed the cattle on green *adduwa* fruit all day and then brought them home at sunset. No sooner had they reached the byre than the biggest bull started singing.

This woman is a bad woman

She fed us green fruit all day

And ate all the ripe fruit herself

This woman is a bad woman

Mend her daughter badly!

The people heard the bull's song. They said to the second wife, "Go into that hut and sleep until morning. We will bring you your daughter at sunrise."

The second wife went into the hut and slept, and in the morning, the people brought her daughter to her. But what a horror she was! One half of her nose was missing, and one arm, and one leg. Half of everything was missing!

The second wife hid her disgust and started on the road home with her daughter. But as soon as they were out of sight of the city, the second wife shouted, "You are not my child!" and ran away.

The second wife tried to hide in some tall grass, but her daughter followed her. When the daughter found her mother, she said, "Come, Mother, let us go home."

But the second wife said, "You are not my child! Leave me alone!"

The daughter replied, "Yes, I am your child, but you are not my mother."

Again the second wife ran away. She ran all the way home, and when she got to her hut, she went inside and closed and barred the door. Eventually her daughter arrived and said, "Open, Mother! I have returned home."

The second wife refused to open the door or even to speak to her daughter. The daughter said again, "Open, Mother! I have returned home."

This time the second wife opened the door. The daughter lived with her mother, and for the rest of her days, the second wife had to deal with the shame of having a disfigured daughter while the first wife's daughter was beautiful.

The Woman and the Children of the Sycamore Tree *(Maasai, Kenya)*

The Maasai of Kenya are known as fierce warriors and cattle rustlers. They live primarily on the meat and milk produced by their cattle, and are one of the largest groups of people living in Kenya. Their traditional lifestyle is nomadic, but in modern times, encroachment on their lands by towns and cities, as well as government prohibitions against living or grazing on protected lands, has forced many of them to settle in villages and give up many of their traditional ways.

In the cautionary tale about the dangers of ingratitude and anger retold below, one of the characters is the Maasai laibon, *or medicine man. The* laibon *has an important place in Maasai culture, functioning as a shaman, healer, and diviner who can give advice to those who need it. The story also centers on the fruit of the sycamore fig, a tree that has been cultivated in the Middle East and Sub-Saharan Africa since ancient times.*

There once was a woman who had lived a long and difficult life. She was very sad because her life had been so hard. She wondered whether perhaps life had been hard for her because she had never married and had never had any children. "I know what I will do," she said to herself. "I will go and ask the laibon to give me a husband and some children. Maybe then my life will be better."

The woman walked all the long way to the laibon's place. When she arrived, the laibon said, "What is it you want of me?"

The woman said, "I have had a long and difficult life. I think it is because I never married and never had children. Can you give me a husband and some children, please?"

The laibon thought for a few moments, then said, "I can give you either a husband or some children. I cannot give you both. You must choose."

"Oh!" said the woman. "I was hoping for both, but if I can only have one, then I would like some children."

"Very well," said the laibon. "If you would like to get some children, you must listen carefully to my instructions and follow them closely. First you must return home and gather up all your cooking pots. You must have at least three, but if you can carry more, that will be even better. Go into the forest and look for a sycamore that is bearing fruit. Fill the pots with as much fruit as they will hold, then put the pots in your house. When all the pots are filled and put away, then you must leave your house and go for a walk. Do not return until sunset."

The woman thanked the laibon and returned home. She gathered up her cooking pots, filled them with sycamore fruit, and put them away in her house. Then she went for a walk. She walked and walked until the sun began to set. She returned home, and as she approached her house, she heard the sound of children's voices. Her home was an astonishing sight. The kraal had been swept clean, the cattle taken out to pasture, the house tidied, and a meal was cooking on the fire. A crowd of children of all ages greeted her. "Mother! Mother!" they cried. "We are so glad you are home. See? We cleaned the house and the kraal, and the boys are out with the cattle. They will bring them home presently."

The woman was overjoyed that she had so many fine children. She lived with them very happily for many days. Then one day, the children did something to displease the woman. Nobody remembers what it was the children did, but everyone remembers what happened afterward. The woman began to scold the children. She said to them, "Oh, you are worthless children! You are nothing but children I got from a sycamore tree! Why should I have expected anything better from a bunch of tree-children?"

The children didn't answer her. They just stood there looking very sad indeed. Then the woman left the house. She went to visit some friends and spent the day with them. While the woman was gone, the children returned to the sycamore tree, where they turned back into fruit.

The woman returned home and saw that her house was empty. She called and called for the children, but they did not answer. A pang of fear went through her body. She ran to the laibon's house and said, "My children have all disappeared! If I put the sycamore fruit into the pots again, will they come back?"

The laibon said, "I don't know. Maybe you should go back to the tree and see whether it tells you what to do."

The woman thanked the laibon and ran home to get her cooking pots. Then she ran into the forest. She ran and ran until she came to the sycamore tree that had given her children before. She climbed up into the tree to pick the fruit that was hanging there, but the skin of every fruit she picked split open, revealing an eye full of tears. No matter where on the tree she took the fruit from, it always had an eye in it.

Finally, the woman realized it was useless. She climbed down from the tree, gathered up her pots, and returned home, weeping bitterly. She spent the rest of her days in sadness and mourning, and never again did she try to get her children back from the sycamore tree.

Part IV: The Influence of Isla

The Story of a Wager *(Tigre, Eritrea)*

The Tigre people of Eritrea are pastoralist nomads who embrace Islam. Arab influence in this EastAfrican country may be seen in the story retold below, which features the character Abunawas. Unlike the characters in most other folktales, Abunawas (d. 814) actually was a historical personage and one of the great poets of Arabic classical literature. Having a reputation that was somewhat larger than life, Abunawas eventually was fictionalized as a trickster character appearing in Arabic folklore including the Arabian Nights collection and many other stories.

Islamic conquerors and Arab traders brought these stories with them when they invaded the eastern coast of Africa, and so the stories worked their way into the folktale repertoire of the African peoples who converted to Islam. Abunawas' role in these tales usually involves tricking greedy, well-off people and showing them the error of their ways, which he does with a great deal of flair in the story retold below.

Once there were two men who made a wager. The first man said to the second, "I will give you all of my cattle if you can stay in the ocean all night long. But if you get out of the water before dawn, you have to give me all of your cattle."

The second said, "I accept your wager."

The second man soon realized that he had acted very foolishly. He thought about what he would have to do and became very frightened. He was sure he would fail and that he would lose all his cattle. He decided to go and ask an old woman he knew to be very wise. He told the woman about the wager and what he had to do, then he said, "Do you know how I might win this bet?"

"Yes, I do," she said. "Ask one of your relatives to go to the seashore with you. They are to build a fire on the beach across from where you will be. They must not let the fire go out at all. While you are in the water, keep your eyes fixed on the flames. That way you will feel warm and will be able to win your wager."

On the night that had been fixed for the wager, the second man and his mother went down to the beach. The mother made a fire, and then the man swam out until he was in deep water and could not touch the bottom. The first man hired watchmen to stand on the beach as well, to make sure that the second man did not come out of the water before daybreak.

And so the night passed, with the second man in the deep water with only his head above the surface, while his mother tended the fire on the beach and the watchmen stood by waiting to see whether the man would come ashore early. When the sun began to rise, the man swam back to the beach and came out of the water. He went to the first man and said, "I have won our wager. I spent the whole night in the ocean and came out alive."

"You have not won anything," said the first man. "My watchmen told me what happened. You were in the water looking at that fire all night. That's how you stayed warm and didn't die."

"How could I have kept warm?" said the second man. "I was so far away from the fire that its heat never reached me at all. Now give me all of your cattle, for I have won our wager."

But the people who were listening to the men agreed that because the second man had been looking at the fire, he hadn't won the bet.

"This will not do," said the second man. "If you will not pay me what you owe, I shall take our case before a judge."

"That is fine with me," said the first man, and so they went before a judge and told him their tale.

When the men were each done telling their side of the story, the judge said, "I find that the wager has been lost, because the man who was in the water looked at the fire all night."

The first man went home happy because he got to keep all of his cattle, but the second was crestfallen. Giving up all of his cattle would mean being ruined forever.

Finally, the second man had an idea. He went to Abunawas, who was a very clever man and had gotten out of many bad situations before. The man told Abunawas his story and how the judge had sided with the first man.

"I know just what to do," said Abunawas. Abunawas sent a messenger throughout the land, inviting everyone to a feast. The first man who had made the wager was invited, and the judge, and the people who had agreed with the first man, and many more besides. Everyone waited impatiently for the feast, for the messenger had told them it would be particularly good.

The day of the feast came, and Abunawas set his servants about slaughtering cattle and goats to make roast meats and stews and making huge pots of rice. But Abunawas said, "You shall not give any of this food to my guests until I tell you to, not even the smallest grain of rice or the smallest piece of meat."

The people came to the feast at the appointed time, and sat down outside Abunawas' house, waiting for the feast to start. Abunawas himself, however, stayed inside his house and said not a word. The servants, meanwhile, set out the food for the guests but did not begin to serve them. The people could see the good food, and smell it, and they said, "Why is Abunawas not serving the food? What kind of feast is this?"

A long time passed. The people became very hungry. But still the servants did not bring them their food. Finally, when the sun was about to set, the people asked one man whom they knew to be a friend of Abunawas to go inside and ask why the feast was not starting.

The friend went inside and said, "Your guests have been waiting all day. They wonder why they have not been served the feast. What shall I tell them?"

Abunawas said, "Go to the people and say, 'You have been smelling the roast meats and the stews and the rice all day, and you have seen them spread out on the table. Surely that should be enough to satisfy you.'"

The friend went back outside and told the people what Abunawas had said. The people became very angry and said, "That makes no sense. How can we be satisfied by food that is far away from us? How does the scent of cooked food satisfy us? How does the sight of cooked food satisfy us?"

Then Abunawas came out of the house and said, "Now you understand that just being able to see or smell something isn't the same as having it. If you can't satisfy your hunger by seeing or smelling cooked food, then neither could the man who spent the night in the sea have been kept warm by looking at a fire that was on the beach."

The people realized that Abunawas was right, and they made the first man pay his debt. When that was done, Abunawas served the feast to all of the people, and when the feast was over, they all went home.

And so it was that Abunawas used his cleverness to help the second man get the payment he was due for winning the wager.

Dschemil and Dschemila *(Berber, Libya)*

"Berber" is not the name of a particular culture but rather is an umbrella term for a group of closely related cultures from North Africa. While most Berbers live in settlements and practice agriculture, some groups, such as the Tuareg, are primarily nomadic. For the most part, Berbers practice Islam, although there is a small Jewish community as well.

In his edition of this story, author and folklorist Andrew Lang notes that he took it from a collection by German linguist Hans Stumme, who collected this and other stories in 1897 in the area around Tripoli. Stumme relied on two informants, one a 45-year-old man named Sidi Brahim ben Xali et-Tekbali, and the other a 15-year-old boy named Mhemmed ben Zumxa Brengali.

This tale follows arcs typical of fairy tales in many cultures. An evil man-eating ogre captures a young woman and turns her into his servant, then the young woman's betrothed comes to rescue her from the ogre's castle, which stands in a remote part of the desert, far from any human habitation. The young people manage to get away using magical objects the young woman steals from her captor. Although the young man struggles somewhat with some of the incidents that follow their escape, he eventually proves his love for his betrothed by honoring her fear that she will be recaptured and doing what is necessary to keep her safe, even if it goes against the traditions of their people.

Once there was a man named Dschemil, and he had a cousin named Dschemila. They had been promised to one another in marriage since they were very small children, but now that they were grown, Dschemil decided that it was time for them to wed. Dschemil, therefore, went to the nearest town to buy furnishings for their new house. The nearest town was quite far away; it took two or three days to get there and another two or three days to come back.

While Dschemil was away, Dschemila and her friends went out to gather firewood. As she picked up sticks, Dschemila came across an iron mortar lying on the ground. She picked it up and fastened it to the top of her bundle, but every time she tried to pick up the bundle to carry it, the mortar fell to the ground. Dschemila undid her bundle to put the mortar in the middle.

Just as Dschemila began to tie up her bundle again, her friends said, "Whatever are you doing over there? It's getting dark, and we're not going to wait for you."

"That's all right," said Dschemila. "You go on ahead. I want to keep this iron mortar I've found. I'll head home as soon as I have it tied up properly in my bundle."

"Very well," said the other young women, who then returned home.

As Dschemila worked to tie up the mortar in her bundle, the sun set. When the last ray of sunlight had gone below the horizon, the iron mortar transformed into a huge ogre. The ogre picked Dschemila up and carried her far, far away to his castle, a whole month's journey from Dschemila's village.

The ogre put Dschemila in a chamber of his castle and said, "Do not be afraid. You will not be harmed." Then the ogre went out, leaving Dschemila sitting in the chamber weeping bitter tears and shivering with fright.

When the other young women of the village returned home, Dschemila's mother noticed that her daughter was not among them.

"Where has my daughter gone?" said the mother. "Why did she not return with you?"

"She found an iron mortar and wanted to tie it up properly to bring it home," said the others. "We expect she'll be back soon."

Dschemila's mother hurried toward the forest to look for her daughter, calling her name all the while. The other villagers saw her and said, "Why don't you go back home? You're just one old woman; this is a job that strong men should be doing."

"Yes, I would welcome help," said the old woman, "but I am coming with you whether you like it or not. My daughter very likely is dead. She probably was bitten by an asp or maybe eaten by a lion."

Once the men understood that the old woman would not stay home, they let her come with them, and together they set out for the forest, taking with them one of the other young women to show where she had last seen Dschemila.

Soon they arrived at the place where Dschemila had been. There they found her bundle of sticks, but no trace of the young woman was to be seen anywhere. They called and called her name, but no one answered.

One of the men said, "Let's light a fire. She will be able to see it even from far away, and then she will know we are looking for her."

The others agreed that this was a good idea, and that while that man kindled the fire, the others should go off in different directions to see whether they could find the girl. They searched and searched all through the night, but they found nothing. When the sun rose, the men said to Dschemila's mother, "We can't find her. We should just go home. Your daughter probably ran off with some man or other."

"Yes, let us go home," said the old woman, "but first I would like to look in the river. Maybe someone threw her in there."

They went and looked in the river, but there was no sign of Dschemila. They all returned home, weary and crestfallen.

Dschemila's mother and father waited anxiously for four days for any news of their daughter, but none ever came. At the end of the fourth day, Dschemila's mother said, "Dschemil will be coming home soon. What are we to tell him?"

"We will tell him she is dead," said the father.

"He will ask to see the grave, and then he will know that something is amiss."

"Tomorrow we will slaughter a goat," said the father. "We will bury its head in the burial ground. We will bring Dschemil there and tell him that that is Dschemila's grave."

The next day, Dschemil arrived with a wagon full of beautiful carpets and cushions to show his bride. He went straight to his in-laws' house, but no sooner had he crossed the threshold than Dschemila's father said, "Greetings. Dschemila is dead."

The young man began to wail and weep. For a long time, he could do nothing else, and he could not speak. When he finally regained his senses, he asked, "Where have you buried her? Please take me to her grave."

The father brought Dschemil to the place where they had buried the goat's head. Dschemil brought along some of the beautiful things he had bought for the new house. He laid them down upon the freshly covered grave and began to weep and mourn. When night fell, he took all the things back to his home, and when day broke, he went back, bringing the things and his flute with him. For six months, he went every day to sit upon what he thought was Dschemila's grave with some of the gifts he had intended to give her, alternately weeping with grief and playing soft, mournful tunes on his flute.

At the time when Dschemil had given himself up to grief, a man was wandering through the desert. The sun was very hot, and the man had run out of water and was very thirsty. He saw before him a great castle, and thought that if only he could rest in the shade, he might find the strength to beg a little water from whoever lived there. He went up to the wall of the castle on the shaded side and sat down to take his ease. It was so lovely and cool in the shade of the castle that he nearly fell asleep, but he startled awake when he heard a soft voice saying, "Who are you? Are you a ghost or a living man?"

The man looked up and saw a girl leaning out of a window.

"I am a man," he said, "and likely a better one than your father or grandfather."

"I wish you good luck," she replied, "but why are you here? This is a land of ogres and all manner of horrible things."

"Is this really the home of an ogre?" asked the man.

"Oh, yes," said the girl. "And as soon as the sun sets, he will come home. If he finds you here, he will turn you into his supper. You need to leave at once, for the day is already getting old."

"I will not get far if I leave without having something to drink," said the man. "I have been journeying all day in the hot desert sun, and I am so thirsty! Please give me some water."

"I can't do that," said the girl, "but if you travel in that direction, you might find a well or a spring. The ogre always goes that way when he wants to get water for the castle."

The man stood up and began to walk away, but the girl called out, "Wait! Tell me where you are going."

"Why do you need to know that?" said the man.

"I have a favor to ask, if you're willing to do it, but I need to know which way you are going."

"I'm going to Damascus," said the man.

"Here is the favor: on your way, you will pass through my village. Ask for a man called Dschemil. Tell him, 'Dschemila is alive and waits for you. She is held captive in a castle out in the desert. Be of good courage.'"

The man promised to take her message, and he walked off in the direction she had shown him. Soon enough, he came across a spring of cool, clear water. The man knelt down and drank and drank until his thirst was quenched. Then he lay down near the spring and slept for a while.

When the man woke up, he said, "That maiden surely did right by me when she told me the way to this spring. I'd be dead if it wasn't for her. I will surely look for her village and take her message to Dschemil."

The man traveled for a whole month, asking at every village he passed through whether there was a man named Dschemil, but everyone always told him there was no one in their village with that name. At the end of that month, the man came to another village. He entered and saw a man sitting in front of one of the houses. The man's hair was long and unkempt, and his beard was shaggy. As the man walked toward the house, the unkempt man said, "Welcome to our village. Where have you come from?"

"I came from the west, and I am walking to the east," said the traveler.

"Come in and take supper with us," said the unkempt man. "You have had a long journey, and you must be hungry."

The traveler went inside, and was made welcome by Dschemila's parents and Dschemil's brothers, who set a meal on the table. All gathered around to eat, and they invited the traveler to partake with them. However, the traveler noticed that one member of the family was missing.

"Where is the unkempt man who invited me into your gracious home?" asked the traveler. "Will he not also eat with us?"

"Don't mind him," whispered one of Dschemil's brothers. "He does that every night. He'll eat something in the morning."

The traveler went on with his meal, wondering what was wrong with the shaggy man. Suddenly one of Dschemil's brothers called out, "Dschemil! Do go and get us some water, if you would."

When the traveler heard the name "Dschemil," he remembered what he had promised the young woman in the castle. "Dschemil!" said the traveler. "Does someone here have that name? I got lost in the desert and came across a castle. There was a maiden in the castle, and she looked out the window and said—"

"Shh!" said one of the brothers. "Don't let him hear you!"

But it was too late. The unkempt man came to the table and said, "Tell me all your tale. Tell me what you saw and what she said. Do it now, or I shall kill you right here."

"I will tell you all, sir," said the traveler. "I was lost in the desert, and before me I saw a castle. I thought to rest in its shade before carrying on with my journey. While I sat with my back against the castle wall, a maiden put her head out of a window above me and asked whether I was man or ghost. I told her I was a man and asked her whether she might give me a drink, for I was very thirsty. She said she had no water to give me, but told me of a spring that was not far off. She also warned me that I needed to leave straight away, for the castle is home to a horrible ogre who might eat me for his supper.

"Before I left, she asked which way I was going. I told her, and she asked a favor of me. She said that I was to find her village and to find the man named Dschemil who lived there, and that when I found him, I was to tell him, 'Dschemila is alive and waits for you. She is held captive in a castle out in the desert. Be of good courage.'"

For a long moment there was silence.

Then the unkempt man, who was indeed Dschemil, said, "Is this true? Is my beloved really still alive?"

The whole family protested that Dschemila was really dead and that the grave was indeed hers.

"We'll see whether you're telling the truth or not," said Dschemil. He snatched up a spade and made to leave for the burial ground.

"Wait!" cried Dschemila's parents. "We'll tell you the truth. Dschemila went out to gather firewood but didn't return with the others. When night fell, we went looking for her, but we couldn't find her anywhere, and she didn't come home. After four days, we decided the best thing to do would be to just tell you that she was dead and make a false grave to convince you that it was true. But since now you know the truth, you should go and find her. Perhaps this man will go with you as a guide; he has been to the castle, and he will be able to show you the way there."

"Yes," said the Dschemil, "that is the best way. Prepare food for my journey while I get my sword."

"Wait," said the traveler. "I don't want to go with you. It took me a whole month to get here, and I have more of my journey left to go, and that's a long way, too."

Dschemil said, "Please come with me for three days to set me on the right path. And after three days, we can each go our separate ways."

"That seems fair," said the traveler, and so they set out on their journey.

For three days Dschemil and his companion traveled from daybreak to dusk, and at dusk of the third day, the traveler said, "Go that way, and walk straight on until you come to a spring. Then keep going in the same direction, and soon enough you will see the castle."

"Very well," said Dschemil. Then the two men said their farewells and parted ways.

Dschemil journeyed on for twenty-six days, and on the evening of the twenty-sixth day, he came across the spring. "This must be the spring the traveler told me about," he said, then he knelt down to take a long drink of the clear, fresh water. When his thirst was quenched, he lay down beside the spring and thought about what he should do next.

"If this is the spring," he thought, "then the castle must be close by. The best thing I can do now is rest, and travel on to the castle in the morning."

And so Dschemil went to sleep there by the spring and slept long and peacefully all night.

Late the next morning, Dschemil awoke. He took another long drink from the spring, then set out to find the castle. It did not take long before he saw it rising out of the desert sand in front of him. "Now to figure out how to get in," Dschemil said. "I can't just knock at the door; surely if I do that, the ogre will grab me and eat me for supper."

Dschemil thought for a while more, then decided the best thing to do would be to climb the wall where maybe he could peep in through a window. He crept up to the castle and began to climb the wall, but no sooner had he arrived at the top than he heard a young woman's voice call out from above him, saying, "Dschemil!"

Dschemil looked up, and what should he see but his beloved Dschemila peeping out of a window above him! Dschemil began to weep for joy.

"My dear beloved one," said the girl, "what brings you here?"

"I came looking for you," he said.

"Oh, no," said Dschemila, "you mustn't. You must leave at once. If the ogre comes home and finds you here, he will kill and eat you!"

"I don't care if there are fifty ogres in this castle," said Dschemil. "I have not grieved for so long and traveled so far just to lose you again."

"If I lowered a rope to you," said Dschemila, "could you use it to climb up and come in through the window?"

"Certainly," the young man replied.

The young woman went back into her chamber. Soon enough, a light rope came down from the window. Dschemil took hold of the rope. He climbed up the rope and went in through the window. When he arrived in Dschemila's chamber, the two young lovers embraced one another tenderly and wept for joy.

"What will we do when the ogre comes back?" asked Dschemila.

"I have a plan," said Dschemil. "Trust me."

Now, Dschemila had a large chest in her chamber, where she kept her clothing and some other things. She had Dschemil get into the chest, and she closed the lid. No sooner had she closed the lid than the ogre came into the chamber, carrying a leg of lamb for Dschemila and two human legs for himself.

"I smell the smell of a man!" roared the ogre. "Where is he?"

"I don't know what you're talking about," said Dschemila. "We're out here in the middle of the desert. There's no one around for miles and miles. How could a man possibly get in here?" Then she burst into tears.

"Oh, my," said the ogre, "I did not mean to upset you. I must be mistaken. Perhaps a raven found some carrion and dropped scraps nearby."

"Yes, that's what happened," said Dschemila. "A raven dropped some bones the other day. I had forgotten."

"That's all right, then," said the ogre. "Go and fetch the bones and burn them into dust. Then put the powder in a cup of water that I may drink them. Bring it to me in the kitchen. You must cook supper for both of us."

Dschemila found some bones, burned them until they turned to dust, then put the powder into a cup of water. She gave this to the ogre, and he drank it. Then he lay down to sleep while Dschemila cooked.

After a little while, the man's legs that were roasting over the fire began to sing,

Ogre, do not rest!

A man is in the chest!

The leg of lamb answered,

That man is your brother

And cousin to this other

The ogre said sleepily, "Who is singing? What did they say?"

"It was only a reminder to add some salt to our dinners," said Dschemila.

"Well, add some salt, then."

"I've already done so."

Then the ogre rolled over and went back to sleep.

No sooner had the ogre fallen back to sleep than the man's legs began to sing,

Ogre, Ogre, do not rest!

A man is in the chest!

The leg of lamb answered,

That man is your brother

And cousin to this other

Again the ogre asked what the voices were saying.

"I need to add pepper this time," said Dschemila.

"Add the pepper, then," said the ogre.

"I've already done so."

The ogre was so very tired that he rolled over and went right back to sleep. A third time the man's legs began to sing.

Ogre, do not rest!

A man is in the chest!

The leg of lamb answered,

That man is your brother

And cousin to this other.

Again the ogre was roused from his sleep. "What did it say this time?" said the ogre.

"It says that it's ready for us to eat."

"Oh, good," said the ogre. "I am very hungry. Please serve me my food."

Dschemila fed the man's legs to the ogre and sliced up the lamb for herself, cleverly hiding some away to give to Dschemil later.

When the ogre finished eating, he washed his hands and then told Dschemila to go to his chamber and make up his bed for him. Dschemila did so, turning down the covers and plumping the pillow for him. The ogre got into bed, and Dschemila tucked him in. Then Dschemila asked, "Father, why do you always sleep with your eyes open?"

The ogre frowned. "Why do you ask? Are you thinking of doing something you shouldn't?"

"Oh, no!" said Dschemila, "I would never do that. I wouldn't even know where to begin, and surely I wouldn't succeed."

"All right, then, but why do you want to know?"

"Well," said Dschemila, "last night I happened to wake up in the middle of the night. The whole castle was shining with a red light. It frightened me, so I wanted to know where that came from and whether you saw it, too."

The ogre chuckled, "Oh, my child, you needn't be afraid of that. The red light happens when I am fast asleep."

"Oh, good," said Dschemila. "I'm glad that that's nothing that could hurt us. But may I ask what is the pin for, the one that you keep next to your bed?"

"The pin turns into an iron mountain if I throw it in front of me."

"Does the darning needle do anything special?"

"Why, yes," said the ogre. "It turns into a big lake."

"What about your hatchet?" said Dschemila.

"The hatchet becomes a thorn hedge so thick and with such long thorns that no one could hope to push through it." The ogre's eyes narrowed, and he looked at Dschemila suspiciously. "But why are you asking me all these questions? It makes me think you are up to no good, and that would make me very angry."

"I only wanted to know what they are for. I see them here all the time, but you never seem to use them. And anyway, where would I go? Who would ever find me here out in the middle of the desert?" And then Dschemila began to cry.

"Please don't cry," said the ogre. "I was only teasing."

"All right," said Dschemila, wiping away her tears. "I'll go to my own bed now. Good night, Father."

"Good night."

Dschemila went back into her chamber and closed the door. She let Dschemil out of the chest.

"Let's go!" said Dschemil. "Let's get out of here now!"

"No, wait," said Dschemila, who went to the door and opened it just a crack. "Do you see that yellow light? It means the ogre isn't asleep yet."

Dschemil and Dschemila waited for an hour. Then Dschemila opened the door a little bit again. There was a red light all over everything. "Look!" she said. "That red light means the ogre is asleep. How shall we escape?"

Dschemil said, "We'll use the rope you let down to me. I'll let you down first, then I'll follow."

"Yes, that is a good plan," said Dschemil. "You get the rope ready. I'm going to get some other things that could help us.

While Dschemil readied the rope, Dschemila crept back into the ogre's bedchamber. She silently took the pin, the darning needle, and the hatchet, and then ran as quickly as she dared back to her chamber. She handed the items to Dschemil and said, "Put these in your pockets. Be careful not to lose them. We may need them later."

"Very well," said Dschemil. Then he tied the rope around Dschemila and let her down. When she was safely on the ground, she untied the rope, and Dschemil used it to climb down himself. Then they both ran away from the castle as fast as they could go.

Now, the ogre slept all through this. He heard nothing when Dschemila came into his chamber and took his things. He heard nothing when the two lovers climbed down the wall. But the ogre had a faithful dog who discovered that Dschemila had escaped. He ran into the ogre's chamber and said, "Why are you sleeping? Dschemila has escaped, and she's running away."

For answer, the ogre kicked the dog, rolled over, and went back to sleep. In the morning, the ogre woke up and called for Dschemila as he usually did, but there was no answer. The ogre went up to Dschemila's chamber and found it empty. He roared with anger, then went downstairs, put on his armor, and picked up his sword. He called his dog and then went out in pursuit of the two lovers.

As Dschemil and Dschemila ran, Dschemila checked over her shoulder every once in a while to see whether the ogre was following them. For a long time, she saw nothing, but soon after daybreak, she looked back and, in the distance, saw the ogre and his dog in hot pursuit.

"The ogre is chasing us!" said Dschemila.

Dschemil looked back and said, "I don't see anything."

"He's there, in the distance. He looks as small as a needle, and he has his dog with him."

The two lovers began to run even faster, but no matter how fast they ran, the ogre still gained on them. When he was nearly upon them, Dschemila said, "Give me the pin, quickly!"

Dschemil gave her the pin, which she threw behind her. Instantly a mountain made out of iron rose up between them and the ogre.

"No matter!" roared the ogre. "We will break this iron into little pieces, and then we will catch you!"

The sound of the ogre and his dog digging and striking at the iron filled the air as Dschemil and Dschemila redoubled their pace. Soon the ogre and his dog had broken through the mountain and once again were catching up to the lovers.

"Dschemil!" cried Dschemila. "Quickly, throw the hatchet behind you!"

Dschemil took the hatchet out of his pocket and threw it over his shoulder. Instantly a hedge made of thorns so thick that no one could ever get through it grew up behind them.

"I may not be able to get through this hedge," roared the ogre, "but I can tunnel underneath!"

The sound of his digging filled the air as the two lovers ran on and on. In what seemed like no time at all, the ogre and his dog were on the other side of the hedge and getting closer and closer to the two young people.

"Dschemil!" cried Dschemila. "Throw the darning needle!"

Dschemil took the darning needle out of his pocket and threw it over his shoulder. Instantly a great lake formed in between the young people and their pursuers.

"Do you think a little bit of water can stop me?" thundered the ogre. "My dog and I will drink this lake dry, and then we will have you!"

The ogre and his dog began to drink the water from the lake. Soon the dog had drunk so much that it burst and died. The ogre realized that he could not finish all the water by himself, so he called out, "Dschemila! May your head become that of a donkey! May your hair turn into a donkey's coat!"

Dschemil turned to look at his cousin and found a strange creature standing next to him. It was wearing Dschemila's clothes, but it had the head and the coat of a donkey, and in the place of hands and feet, it had hooves. Dschemil took a step back in horror and said, "You were never my cousin. You were a little donkey-creature the entire time!" Dschemil ran away from the creature and went back to his own village.

Dschemila wandered about the desert all alone for two days, weeping all the while. Meanwhile, Dschemil had nearly arrived back at his village. He couldn't stop thinking about what had happened. He began to feel ashamed of himself for having abandoned the donkey. "What if it really was Dschemila after all?" he thought. "What if the ogre's spell has worn off? I can't leave her alone in the desert."

Dschemil turned back in search of his cousin. After a time, he found her, still with a donkey's head and coat, perched on top of a rock and surrounded by wolves. Dschemil drove the wolves away and helped his cousin down from the rock.

"Well, that was close," said Dschemil. "Those wolves would have had you if I hadn't come along."

Dschemila glared at her cousin. "Those wolves wouldn't have been anywhere near me if you had just taken me home."

"I thought you were a witch!" said Dschemil. "You turned into a donkey, right before my eyes!"

"Yes, I turned into a donkey," said Dschemila, "because the ogre cast a spell on me!"

"What did you expect me to do?" said Dschemil. "What would everyone have said if I came home leading a half-woman, half-donkey and said, 'Behold, I have rescued Dschemila?'"

"What are you going to do now?" said Dschemila.

"I don't know."

"Why don't you take me home at night? Just bring me to my mother's house, and I'll do the rest."

They waited next to the rocks until the sun had set, then journeyed back to the village. When they arrived, they went to Dschemila's mother's house and knocked on the door.

"Who is there?" the mother said.

"It is I, Dschemil."

The mother opened the door, and Dschemil said, "I found Dschemila, and I've brought her home."

The mother looked at the little donkey and said, "Since when have I been the mother of a donkey? That is not my daughter. You need to leave right now. This is foolishness."

"Hush!" said Dschemil. "Do you want to wake the whole village? This really is Dschemila. She's under a spell."

Dschemila sobbed. "Mother, it really is me. Do you not know me?"

"Do you remember that Dschemila had two scars?" said Dschemil.

"Yes, she had one on her thigh from a dog bite," said the mother, "and another on her breast from a burn with lamp oil that she got when she was small."

Dschemila took off her clothes and showed the two scars to her mother. When the mother saw that this indeed was her daughter, she embraced her joyfully, and they both wept. "Oh, daughter," said the mother, "who did this to you?"

"It was the ogre, Mother," said Dschemila. "He captured me when I was in the forest gathering firewood, and he kept me in his castle. Then Dschemil rescued me, but the ogre put a spell on me while we were escaping."

"I am very glad you are home and safe, but what are we going to tell everyone?" said the mother.

"Hide me here in your home," said Dschemila. "And Dschemil, if anyone asks whether you found me, keep pretending that I'm still lost. I'll take care of the rest."

The mother hid Dschemila in her home, and Dschemil returned to his family.

"Welcome home!" said Dschemil's father. "Did you find your cousin?"

"No, not a trace. I looked everywhere."

"What happened to the man who went with you?" said Dschemil's brother.

"After three days I had to let him leave. He was useless. He's probably arrived at his own home by now. I searched every castle I could find, but there was no sign of Dschemila anywhere."

"Ah, well," said Dschemil's father. "She probably got snatched by an ogre who ate her for his supper. Not much one can do about that."

Even after Dschemil repeated this story many times, people still kept asking him whether he was going to go look for Dschemila again, and every time he said he was not.

"All right then," said his friends and family, "we'll just have to find you someone else to be your wife. There are many beautiful girls in this village who would be pleased to marry you. Choose one."

But every time, Dschemil said he would have none other but his cousin. The people of the village began to think him mad. "You went out and bought all those furnishings, and now they're just sitting around unused. Choose another girl! Marry, and be happy!"

"I will never marry anyone other than my beloved Dschemila," said Dschemil. "Stop asking me!"

Three months went by. Then one day a merchant drew near to the ogre's castle. He went to sit in the shade of the wall, and the ogre found him there.

"What are you doing near my castle?" said the ogre.

The man stood up, trembling with fear.

"Please, sir, I am only a merchant. See? This is my bundle of goods. I sell clothing."

"Don't be afraid," said the ogre. "I won't eat you. At least not yet. I need your help."

"What do you want me to do?" said the merchant.

"Go in that direction," said the ogre, "and after a few days, you will come to a village. Take this comb and mirror, and ask the people of the village whether they know a young woman named Dschemila and a young man named Dschemil. When you find the young woman, give her the comb and the mirror and tell her, 'Your father the ogre bids you look in this mirror, and your own face will be returned to you. Then comb your coat with this comb, and all will be restored to you as it was before.'"

"I will do everything you say," said the merchant.

"That is good," said the ogre, "because if you don't, I will eat you for sure."

After a long journey, the merchant arrived at Dschemila's village. He sat down as soon as he could find a good spot, because he was tired, hungry, and very, very thirsty. Dschemil came upon him sitting there and said, "You really should get out of the sun. You will get sunstroke if you stay there."

"Yes, thank you," said the merchant, "but I have been traveling for a whole month, and I am too tired and hungry and thirsty to move right now."

"From where did you come?"

The merchant pointed in the direction of the ogre's castle. "That way," he said.

"Did you see anything interesting on your travels?" asked Dschemil.

"I did indeed. I came across a castle, and the ogre there told me to look for a young woman called Dschemila and a young man called Dschemil. Do those people live here?"

"I am Dschemil. What does the ogre want?"

"He gave me gifts to give to the young woman," said the merchant.

"Come with me," said Dschemil, and he led the merchant to his aunt and uncle's house.

When they arrived, Dschemila's mother asked, "Who is this man, and what does he want?"

"I am a merchant, ma'am, and I am looking for a young woman named Dschemila. An ogre sent me to look for her. He asked me to give her this comb and this mirror."

"It's a trick," said the mother. "Surely that ogre is only trying to harm my daughter further."

"I'm not sure that it's a trick," said Dschemil. "I think we should try."

Dschemila's mother called her daughter out of her hiding place and told her about the merchant. Dschemila went to the merchant and said, "I hear the ogre sent you with some things for me."

"Yes," said the merchant. "He sent me with this comb and this mirror, and he told me that I was to say that your father the ogre sent these to you, and that you were to look into the mirror and comb your coat with the comb, and that if you did that, you would become as you used to be."

Dschemila took the mirror and looked into it, and she combed her coat with the comb. When she was done, in place of a creature that looked like a donkey, there stood a beautiful young woman. Dschemila's mother and cousin rejoiced greatly to see the young woman restored. Soon word went through the village that Dschemila had returned. Everyone wanted to know when she got back, but all she would say was, "Dschemil brought me, but I didn't want to reveal myself right away. I wanted to wait until the time felt right."

Then Dschemil said to his parents and brothers and in-laws, "Let us have the wedding today. We have waited so long, but now Dschemila is here and we can be married."

The villagers prepared a beautiful litter to carry the bride to her new home, but Dschemila would not ride in it. "What if the ogre sees me?" she said. "Surely he will come and take me away again."

The men of the village said, "We wouldn't let him come near you. There are many of us, and we all have swords."

"It doesn't matter how many you are or how sharp your swords," said Dschemila. "That ogre is ruthless and cunning. I know him."

One old man said, "We should listen to her. If she won't ride the litter to her new house, maybe she can walk."

The others protested that the ogre couldn't possibly take her away again, but Dschemila would not be swayed. She would neither ride the litter nor walk. Soon it looked like an argument would break out, but Dschemil said, "If she is too afraid to leave this house, then I will live here with her. We can still have the wedding feast, and Dschemila will feel safe and cared for."

And so Dschemil and Dschemila were finally made man and wife, and they lived together in great peace and happiness to the end of their days.

Part 2: Egyptian Gods

A Captivating Guide to Atum, Horus, Seth, Isis, Anubis, Ra, Thoth, Sekhmet, Geb, Hathor and Other Gods and Goddesses of Ancient Egypt

Introduction

It is tempting to see ancient Egyptian religion as something relatively static, with a single pantheon whose nature and activities did not change throughout the three-thousand-year span of the Dynastic Period. However, nothing could be further from the truth. Throughout Egyptian history, we see that gods who had once been favored were set aside or had their roles altered in order to make way for gods whose cults became more popular, while political changes, such as the conquest of Egypt by Alexander the Great, ushered in cultural and religious exchanges that both affected native Egyptian religious practices and also had an impact on the religious beliefs of Greece and Rome.

Fluidity was built into the structure of Egyptian religion itself. Many gods and goddesses had special relationships with other deities, often taking on aspects of those gods, such that a new, syncretized deity was created. We see this especially with the god Amen and the goddess Bastet. Amen's association with the sun god, Ra, created the syncretized deity Amen-Ra, and in this guise, Amen became the supreme deity of Egypt during the New Kingdom. Bastet, on the other hand, was not combined with a second deity but rather was seen to be the calm, affectionate avatar of the lion-headed goddess Sekhmet, who once went on a rampage and tried to kill all humankind. Sekhmet, in turn, was considered to be a violent manifestation of the cow-headed goddess, Hathor.

Syncretization was not the only way in which relationships were established or changed between and among Egyptian deities. For example, it sometimes can be difficult to establish which deity was the consort or child of which other god or goddess, since these groupings could shift depending on location and time period. For example, the god Khnum, who had his major cult centers in southern Egypt near the source of the Nile, was variously made the husband of the goddesses Satis, Menhit, and Neith, while the god Khonsu was worshiped as the son of Amen and Mut in southern Egypt, as the son of Ptah and Sekhmet in the north, or as the son of Hathor and Sobek in the Temple of Kom Ombo in central Egypt.

The importance of the family bond to ancient Egyptians is reflected in their preference for making collections of deities that represent family groupings. For example, the Heliopolitan Ennead (Nine Gods) represented four generations of the same family. More commonly, however, these groupings were of a single nuclear family of two parents and one child, usually referred to as a "triad." Although a temple might be dedicated to a single god such as Horus, that temple did not neglect to include both the god's consort and son or daughter although, as mentioned above, exactly which deities were grouped into which triads might vary depending on the historical period and location.

There are multiple ancient Egyptian creation myths, and which creation story a particular person accepted as true might depend on where they were from. For example, the major religious centers of Hermopolis, Thebes, and Memphis each had their own creation myth, and although some deities, such as Thoth, cross over from one cosmogony to the other, these tales are largely independent of one another. The three cities mentioned above were all large and important, but status was not necessary in order for a place to have its own creator god and creation myth. We see this with the ram-headed god Khnum, whose main cult centers were far from the seats of power, and who was considered to be the creator of the universe by the people who worshiped him in his shrines on the island of Elephantine and at Esna.

Because the pharaohs were deemed to be the sons of a deity (variously Horus the Younger or Amen-Ra, depending on the historical period), Egyptian religion was closely allied with politics. The pharaoh had the power to create and endow temples for the worship of the gods, and a pharaoh's particular religious enthusiasms could cause shifts in national religious beliefs and practices. We see these kinds of changes especially during the New Kingdom. For example, when Pharaoh Ahmose I defeated the invading Hyksos, who had taken over Egypt, he claimed that his victory was the result of Amen's favor. Pharaohs thereafter declared themselves the sons of Amen-Ra. This caused a surge in the popularity of Amen's cult, for which the vast temple complex at Karnak was constructed. Similarly, during the reign of the Ptolemies, interest in the goddess Isis increased the number of devotees to her cult, which spread beyond the boundaries of Egypt into Greece and Rome.

Pharaohs could also change (or at least attempt to change) religious practice by fiat. Pharaoh Akhenaten is perhaps the best known for this, having declared traditional worship banned in favor of his own monotheistic system that centered on the sun god Aten. Akhenaten's heresy was heavily resented by his people and did not outlast his own regime; his reforms were reversed by his son, Tutankhamun.

Changes instituted by other monarchs had considerably more staying power, however. This was particularly true of Ptolemy I's creation of the new deity Serapis. Serapis was considered to be the consort of Isis and was a syncretization of the god Osiris and the Apis bull. He had some Greek characteristics and was an attempt on the part of the Greek pharaoh to create commonalities between Greeks and Egyptians living under his rule.

Because the Egyptian pantheon is vast, even if one leaves out the syncretized deities, it is not possible for this volume to present a comprehensive overview of ancient Egyptian religion and myth. Instead, only a select number of deities and concepts are discussed here. Some of these are more well-known deities, while others might not be as familiar to modern readers. However, this book still offers a fascinating glimpse into ancient Egyptian religion and culture and the richness that was life in ancient Egypt.

Timeline of Ancient Egypt

This brief timeline of the history of ancient Egypt includes notes on historical characters that are either well known or are mentioned in the text. Dates are regnal dates unless otherwise noted.

Period	Dynasties	Dates
Archaic Period	1–2	c. 3000–2650 BCE
Hor-Aha (no definite dates)		
Old Kingdom	3–8	c. 2650–2135 BCE
Djoser, second half of 26th century BCE (dates unclear)		
Khafre, 2558–2532 BCE		
Unas, 2375–2345 BCE		
Teti, 2345–2323 BCE		
Pepi I, 2321–2184 BCE		
First Intermediate Period	9–11	c. 2135–2040 BCE

Middle Kingdom	11–14	c. 2040–1650 BCE

Amenemhet I, 1985–1955 BCE

Senusret I, 1965–1920 BCE

Senusret III, 1880–1855 BCE

Amenemhet III, 1855–1808 BCE

Hyksos Period/ Second Intermediate Period	15–17	c. 1650–1550 BCE

The Hyksos were foreign invaders, possibly from Western Asia

New Kingdom	18–20	c. 1550–1080 BCE

Ahmose I, 1550–1525 BCE

Thutmose II, 1492–1479 BCE

Hatshepsut, 1479–1458 BCE

Thutmose III, 1479–1425 BCE

Thutmose IV, 1479–1390 BCE

Amenhotep III, 1390–1352 BCE

Amenhotep IV / Akhenaten, "The Heretic King," 1353–1336 BCE

Tutankhamun, 1336–1327 BCE

Rameses II, r. 1279–1212 BCE

Late Period	21–31	c. 1080–332 BCE

The Late Period saw repeated incursions by outside rulers:

25th Dynasty (780–656 BCE): Cushite rulers

Taharqa, 690–664 BCE

27th Dynasty (525–404 BCE): Persian rulers

28th-30th Dynasty (404-341 BCE): Egyptian pharaohs

NECTANEBO II, 360-342 BCE

31st Dynasty (342-332 BCE): return of Persian rule

Alexander the Great (332-323 BCE)

Ptolemaic Period	**323-30 BCE**

Rule by Macedonian Greeks after the death of Alexander

Ptolemy I Soter, 305-285 BCE

Cleopatra VII Philopator, 51-30 BCE

Roman Period	**30 BCE-395 CE**

Egypt annexed as part of the Roman Empire

Augustus, 31 BCE-14 CE

Tiberius, 14-37 CE

Caligula, 37-41 CE

Vespasian, 69-79 CE

Hadrian, 117-138 CE

Amen (Amun, Amon, Ammon)

Amen is an excellent example of the complexities of Egyptian religion, in the ways that religion changed across time, in how it was tied to local practice, and the ways in which it intersected with and was affected by politics in the Dynastic Period. Amen's two earliest manifestations were at Thebes and Hermopolis. In Thebes, Amen functioned as the main creator god of the city, having supplanted an earlier god named Montu, while in Hermopolis, he was one of the eight deities of the Ogdoad, a collection of four male and four female deities who created the universe and who were considered to be personifications of various important abstract concepts such as darkness or infinity. In Hermopolis, Amen, along with his consort Amaunet, was considered to be the personification of hiddenness, since his name literally means "hidden one" or "invisible." As such, he was associated with air and the wind.

There are several versions of the Hermopolitan creation myth, which is discussed in the chapter on the Ogdoad below. The Theban cosmogony makes use of the theme of the cosmic egg, which it has in common with some versions of the Hermopolitan myth. In the Theban myth, Amen hatches uncreated out of an egg that sits on the primeval mound; after this happens, he goes on to create the rest of the world. Thebes proudly asserted that the city was built on this primeval mound, thus asserting itself as the center of creation and the place of Amen's first emergence into being.

In Thebes, Amen became combined with the solar deity Ra, creating one all-powerful god called Amen-Ra. Other syncretizations of Amen joined him with Min, the god of fertility and virility, and with Ptah, another creator god whose main cult center was in Memphis. However, it was as Amen-Ra in the city of Thebes that Amen gained his greatest importance, both in terms of religious worship and in his connections to Egyptian political power.

Amen gained prestige and importance, and as Amen-Ra, he eventually became the principal god of Egypt during the New Kingdom. One reason for Amen's ascendancy from a secondary, local god of the city of Thebes to a national, all-powerful deity was the defeat of the Hyksos by Ahmose I. The Hyksos were immigrants to Egypt who gradually were able to seize considerable political power, especially in the southern part of the country, where Thebes is located. The period of Hyksos rule is known as the Second Intermediate Period. When Ahmose I defeated the Hyksos and drove them out of Egypt, he claimed that his victory was due to the favor of Amen, giving Amen a considerable boost in popularity and power, allowing Amen to supplant Montu, a war god who had been the main deity of Thebes up to that point.

As a national deity, Amen was said to be the husband of Mut, a sky goddess, and the father of Khonsu, the god of the moon. Together, these three deities were known as the Theban Triad, and they were worshiped at the massive temple complex at Karnak, one of the largest and most elaborate ancient Egyptian religious centers.

The newly syncretized god of Thebes, Amen-Ra, was given the role of father of the pharaoh, a shift from earlier times when the pharaoh was thought to be the son of Horus. Historian Samuel Kramer notes that, in this guise, Amen-Ra began to take on many of the characteristics now generally associated with the concept of God as elucidated in the Bible.[1] Like God, Amen-Ra was seen as an uncreated being who, through his own unlimited power, created the universe. Amen-Ra also subjugated the other gods under his power, was invisible and everywhere, and was able to manifest himself in various ways to humankind.

We see this concept of Amen-Ra as the all-powerful and one true god in a hymn written for Pinedjem II, the high priest of Amen-Ra from 990 to 969 BCE:

> This venerable god, Lord of all Gods, Amon-Re, Lord of the Throne(s) of the Two Lands, He who resides in He who Reckons the Thrones.
>
> Venerable manifestation which came into being in the beginning, Great God who lives on Truth, first Primeval One who engendered the primeval gods, out of whom all the other gods came into being.
>
> The Unique One, who created what exists at the first beginning of the earth. Mysterious of births, of numerous appearances, whose manifestations are not known.
>
> Venerable Power, beloved and feared, rich of appearances, Lord of Might, creative power, out of whose form came into being every form, he who came first into being, besides whom nothing exists.

---

[1] Samuel Noah Kramer, *Mythologies of the Ancient World* (Garden City: Doubleday, 1961), 47.

He who gave light to the earth, for
the first time with the disk. Light,
Radiating One, when he appears, men
live. When he sails the sky, he is not
weary, early in the morning his work is
already fixed.[2]

Although we can see how the character of Amen-Ra resonates with
that of the biblical God in this hymn, we can also see some of the
ways that Amen-Ra remains distinct. Amen-Ra may have been the
supreme god of the Egyptians, but he was not the sole god, and his
aspect as the god of the sun remains intact, as we see in the last verse,
which refers specifically to the rising of the sun ("the disk") and its
course across the sky during the day.

As the supreme god of Egypt, Amen-Ra was given pride of place
through the construction of the great temple complex at Karnak.
Although construction of the temple complex began in the Middle
Kingdom during the reign of Senusret I, the bulk of it was built
during the New Kingdom by Pharaoh Amenhotep III. The temple of
Amen at Karnak is considered to be one of the largest religious
structures in the world, and its hypostyle hall (an unroofed area made
of multiple colossal pillars) and the giant, hieroglyphic-encrusted
papyrus columns leading up to the entrance are images immediately
recognizable to many people today.

This elevation of Amen-Ra to supreme god had political
repercussions, both through the more widespread worship of Amen-
Ra and through the symbol of his cult's visible temporal power at
Karnak. Although many other temples to Amen-Ra were constructed
at this time, the magnificence and sheer size of the Karnak temple
gave it considerable status. The other factor in the cult's political
ascendency was the alliance of the priesthood of Amen-Ra with the
monarchy.

---

[2] Translation in Alexandre Piankoff, trans., and Natacha Rambova, ed.,
   Mythological Papyri: Texts (New York: Pantheon Books, 1957), 18.

This alliance began with the defeat of the Hyksos. As Samuel Kramer observes, when Ahmose I attributed his victory to Amen, he effectively shackled himself and his successors with a debt of gratitude that was expressed through the granting of land, treasure, and slaves to the priesthood of Amen as tangible signs of the king's thanks for Amen's protection.[3] As with so many endeavors that seem like a good idea at the time, the enrichment of the priesthood of Amen-Ra eventually proved disastrous for the pharaohs, because it siphoned power away from the monarchy and gave it to the priests. The Amen-Ra priesthood effectively became kingmakers because, as Kramer reports,

> the god's role as father of the king gave the priests considerable strength in selecting and supporting a particular candidate for the kingship.... Thus, by expressing or withholding divine approval, the priests of Amon-Re' [*sic*] could ensure their candidate was successful.[4]

Through their vast wealth and religious control over who might legitimately sit on the throne, the priesthood of Amen functioned in many ways as the *de facto* rulers of Egypt by the time of Amenhotep III.

However, it was not only the male heirs to the throne who claimed to be the children of Amen-Ra. When Queen Hatshepsut assumed the title of pharaoh upon the death of her husband, Thutmose II, she had an official myth created that claimed her birth to be ordained by none other than Amen-Ra himself. In the myth, Amen-Ra tells the assembled company of the gods that he wants to make a queen to rule over all of Egypt. He sends out Thoth to find a woman to be the mother of this great queen, and when she is located, Amen-Ra impregnates her, and thus Hatshepsut is conceived. But Amen-Ra isn't done; he commissions the god Khnum, the ram-headed god of

---

[3] Kramer, Mythologies of the Ancient World, 124.
[4] Kramer, Mythologies of the Ancient World, 124.

the Nile floods, to make Hatshepsut's body and soul on his potter's wheel. In this project, Khnum is helped by the goddess Hekt, a fertility goddess also associated with the flooding of the Nile. Thus, not only was Hatshepsut the daughter of Amen-Ra, but her very body and soul were created by the gods at Amen-Ra's command.

Hatshepsut needed this myth in order to promote the legitimacy of her rule, because she originally took the throne not as the direct heir of the pharaoh but rather as the dowager queen regent to her infant son, who later became Thutmose III. In Hatshepsut, we see how a ruler might manipulate the power of Amen-Ra's cult in order to further her own political ambitions, which stands in stark distinction to the situation under later pharaohs, who essentially were under the thumbs of Amen-Ra's priests.

Alexander the Great was another ruler who seized upon the popularity of Amen-Ra in order to legitimize his own rule. When Alexander conquered Egypt in 331 BCE, he claimed that he was the son of Ammon-Zeus, a syncretization of the Greek supreme god Zeus with the Egyptian Amen. Amen was also adopted by the Romans as Ammon-Jupiter.

The primary challenge to the power of Amen-Ra and his priests came during the rule of Amenhotep IV. Sometimes known as the "heretic king," Amenhotep changed his name to Akhenaten in the fifth year of his reign and began a series of sweeping religious reforms intended to shift all worship to a single solar deity, Aten. Akhenaten's reforms are discussed in detail in the chapter on Aten below.

The national worship of Amen was weakened somewhat because of Akhenaten's reforms, and it further waned during the tenth century BCE, although his cult remained important in Thebes. Amen was eclipsed particularly during the Ptolemaic Period, when Isis and Serapis became a central focus of worship not only in Egypt but also in many communities in Greece and Rome. Amen's cult was not erased entirely until Christianity was established as a state religion in the mid-fifth century CE.

Anubis (Anpu, Inpw)

With his black jackal's head perched upon a man's body, Anubis is one of the most easily identified ancient Egyptian deities. Some depictions of this god show him holding the ankh, or symbol of life, in one hand and a staff in the other, while other images show him tending to the dead body of a pharaoh. This association with death and decay is one of Anubis's chief characteristics. Indeed, his name in Egyptian, *Anpu*, literally means "decay" ("Anubis" is the Greek form of the name), and it is possible that the use of the jackal's head as one of the attributes of this god may be a reference to the tendency of jackals to scavenge in cemeteries and other places where dead bodies are found.

Although Anubis was always considered to be a god of death and the dead, his position within Egyptian religion altered over time. During the First Dynasty, Anubis was the primary god of the dead, but this changed during the Middle Kingdom, when the cult of Osiris gained popularity and Osiris was elevated to the supreme god of the dead and lord of the Tuat, the ancient Egyptian Underworld. Anubis may have lost his throne to Osiris, but he did not lose his importance; instead, his role shifted from ruler of the dead to embalmer and judge.

The myths surrounding Anubis's origins and parentage also changed over time. In some early myths, Anubis is said to be the son of the sun god Ra and the brother of Osiris, Isis, Nephthys, and Set, either by the sky goddess Nut or the cow-headed goddess Hesat. In later myths, he is considered to be the son of Nephthys, who tricked Osiris into having intercourse with her. This shift likely had to do with the increasing importance of the Osiris cult and the need to incorporate Anubis into a new mythical and religious framework that centered on Osiris, rather than Anubis, as the god of the dead.

One of Anubis's chief duties in the Tuat was the judging of souls to see whether or not they were worthy of eternal life. When the soul of a deceased person came before Anubis, Anubis weighed their heart against the feather of truth. The deceased person then had to vow that they had lived a good life full of good deeds. If the person was telling the truth, the heart would weigh less than the feather, and the person would be allowed into the delights of the afterlife. If the person was lying, however, the heart would weigh more than the feather, and the person would be condemned to obliteration by being devoured by Ammit, a goddess with the head of a crocodile, the forequarters of a lion, and the hindquarters of a hippopotamus.

Anubis was also the god of embalming, a role that became important after the rise of the Osiris cult. When Isis finds Osiris's dead body, Anubis helps her embalm it and wrap it in linen wrappings. The other part of the embalming process was the preservation of the stomach, intestines, lungs, and liver, which were placed into jars made of earthenware, alabaster, or other hard, non-porous materials. These jars sometimes had stoppers carved or molded into the likeness of gods who had the responsibility for looking after these organs, which the deceased person was believed to get back after death. This tradition of preserving the organs also comes from the Osiris myth, since Anubis was given Osiris's organs after Osiris died.

As with several other gods in the Egyptian pantheon, Anubis became absorbed into Greco-Roman religious practices during the Ptolemaic Period. Anubis was often syncretized with the Greek god Hermes, who had the task of conducting souls to Hades. In this way, Anubis gained a function as a guide of souls in addition to his other duties as embalmer, judge of the dead, and protector of tombs and cemeteries.

Ancient Egyptian writings that mention Anubis include the Pyramid Texts, which are inscriptions inside a series of Old Kingdom pyramids that were built for five pharaohs and some of their wives. These texts, which preserve spells and prayers intended to raise the occupant of the tomb from the dead and guide them to eternal life, place Anubis in various roles with respect to the deceased. Some of the spells suggest that the dead person would themselves become Anubis in some way, while others refer to the god's duties as embalmer and the guide and transformer of souls. Below are some examples from the tomb of Pharaoh Pepi I:

> Awake for Horus, stand up against Seth! Raise yourself as Osiris, as the akh [soul] who is Geb's first son, and take up your position as Anubis on the shrine.[5]

> So, [Pepi] will go forth to the sky, his wingtips those of a big bird. His entrails have been washed by Anubis, and Horus's service in Abydos—Osiris's purification—has been performed.[6]

---

[5] James P. Allen, *The Ancient Egyptian Pyramid Texts* (Atlanta: Society of Biblical Literature), 105.

[6] Allen, *Pyramid Texts*, 158. Abydos refers to the ancient Egyptian city by that name, where a royal necropolis was located. Bracketed insert is mine.

Anubis, foremost of the god's
booth, has commanded that you
descend as a star, as the morning god.[7]

Your akh is about [you, father
Osiris Pepi], as a king-given offering
that shall exist for you as one that
Anubis made for you.[8]

In these texts, it is Anubis himself who embalms the pharaoh and
who transforms him into a divine being, a process that includes the
pharaoh taking on the identity of Anubis for himself. The last section
of the text also suggests that the soul of the pharaoh—likely in its
resurrected state—is something created specifically for the pharaoh by
Anubis.

Anubis had a presence and a function outside of funerary texts
and royal burials, however. "The Tale of Two Brothers," an Egyptian
folktale from the New Kingdom, tells the story of Anubis and Bata,
brothers who initially live in the same household together, along with
Anubis's wife. In this story, Bata acts as a herdsman and worker on
Anubis's land. All goes well until Anubis's wife tries to seduce Bata.
When Bata refuses her advances, she pretends that he has assaulted
her. Anubis initially believes his wife's story, and Bata barely escapes
with his life. As part of his oath to Anubis that he is telling the truth,
Bata cuts off his penis and throws it into the river. He then runs into
the wilderness, where he builds a house for himself. He places his
heart at the top of an acacia tree that grows nearby.

The gods see that Bata is living alone and so provide a wife for
him. Bata tells her not to leave the house, because the sea desires her
and will snatch her away. When the wife disobeys Bata, the sea tries
to abduct her, but the woman runs too fast and manages to get safely
back into the house. As the woman is running away, the sea tells the

---

[7] Allen, *Pyramid Texts*, 168.
[8] Allen, *Pyramid Texts*, 195. Bracketed insert in the original.

acacia tree to grab her, but the tree only manages to get a lock of her hair, which falls into the water.

The hair floats down the river to the place where the pharaoh's launderers are doing the wash. The pharaoh's clothing picks up the scent of Bata's wife's perfume, and the pharaoh commands the woman to be brought to him. When she arrives, she becomes the pharaoh's wife, and she soon tells the pharaoh about the acacia tree that holds Bata's heart. The pharaoh commands that the tree be destroyed. Cutting down the tree kills Bata.

Anubis is alerted to Bata's death by certain signs. Anubis then goes looking for his brother and finds Bata's dead body on the bed inside his house. Bata had told Anubis that his heart was to be stored outside of his body, so Anubis goes looking for it. After a long search, he finds the heart and restores it to Bata's body, which brings Bata back to life. Bata then transforms himself into a magical bull and tells Anubis to ride him to the court of the pharaoh.

Bata's former wife, who is still living at the royal court as the wife of the pharaoh, learns that her husband has transformed himself into a bull and means to get revenge on her, so she arranges for the bull to be sacrificed and cut into pieces. However, her plans are foiled when two drops of the bull's blood land outside the doors of the temple. From this blood, two trees sprout up, one of which accuses the woman of treachery as she sits in its shade.

Bata's former wife arranges for the trees to be cut down and chopped up, but a splinter from the tree that spoke to her goes into her mouth and impregnates her. For a second time, Bata is brought back from the dead, for the infant borne by Bata's former wife is Bata himself, who goes on to become pharaoh. The story ends with Bata pronouncing judgment on his former wife and making Anubis his heir.

Although Bata was a New Kingdom god in his own right, it is easy to see the parallels between his story and the myth of the dying and rising Osiris, as well as between the role of Anubis in this story and his functions elsewhere in Egyptian myth. Bata clearly plays the role of Osiris; his severed penis ends up in a river, and he is brought back to life after having died through the ministrations of Anubis. Like Osiris, Bata becomes imprisoned in the wood of a tree, and he later is restored to full life a second time, after which he comes into his power as the lord of the land.

Just as the adventures of Bata represent the journey of Osiris from life to death to resurrection to kingship, so, too, does Anubis maintain his traditional funerary role in this tale. It is Anubis's duty to find and tend to the body of the dead Bata and to restore him to life through his magic by placing Bata's heart back in his body. This parallels Anubis's work in helping to embalm the dead Osiris, thus restoring him to life. Anubis also acts as a sort of guide for Bata when Bata takes on the form of a bull, and when Bata enters into his authority as pharaoh, Anubis is given an important role as the crown prince of the realm, just as Anubis was given important authority in the Tuat under the kingship of Osiris.

Anubis's association with death and judgment, as well as the imposing image of his black jackal's head and muscular body, often lead modern people to see him as a fearsome and potentially violent god. However, as we have seen, ancient Egyptian people did not view Anubis that way. For the ancient Egyptians, Anubis was a god who tenderly cared for the dead and whose gifts and power allowed the souls of the just to enter eternal life.

Aten (Aton)

The god Aten was identified with the sun disk and was considered to be a creator god who made all things and who sustained the universe by his power. Because the Egyptian word "aten" means "disk," this god is sometimes referred to as "the Aten," or "the sun disk." The earliest depictions of the Aten show it as a man with a falcon's head, but eventually the Aten came to be depicted as the sun giving off many rays or as a disk with outstretched wings. These depictions reflect the understanding of Aten as a god of light who is everywhere, who cannot be defined by a particular form, and whose *ba*, or spiritual essence, cannot be represented by an earthly animal.

Worship of Aten is most commonly associated with the reign of Pharaoh Amenhotep IV, who took the name Akhenaten and who attempted to elevate the Aten cult above all others. However, worship of the sun disk as an all-powerful god actually began before Akhenaten took the throne. As Egyptologist George Hart states, "The worship of Aten was not a sudden innovation on the part of one king, but the climax of a religious quest among Egyptians for a benign god limitless in power and manifest in all countries and all natural phenomena."[9]

---

[9] George Hart, *A Dictionary of Egyptian Gods and Goddesses* (London:

Akhenaten's royal transference of the worship of Amen-Ra to the worship of Aten, not only as the primary deity but as the sole god of Egypt, had some of its roots in religious and political changes that had taken place hundreds of years earlier, with Ahmose I's defeat of the Hyksos and the elevation of the cult of Amen-Ra, which in turn greatly increased the power of Amen-Ra's priests. Declaring a different god to be both supreme and the primary patron of the pharaoh had the effect of gutting the authority of Amen-Ra's priesthood and restoring to the pharaohs some of their lost power.

The earliest mention of the Aten as a divine concept, if not a separate deity in its own right, extends back to the Middle Kingdom. We find this in an ancient Egyptian tale known as "The Story of Sinuhe," a first-person narrative purportedly written by a highly placed official at the court of the pharaoh. Early in the narrative, Sinuhe announces the death of the Twelfth Dynasty pharaoh Amenemhet I, who died in 1955 BCE. Sinuhe says, "He [the pharaoh] penetrated the sky, being joined to the sun disk [the Aten], the God's body being mixed with that of him who made him."[10]

Increasing reverence for the Aten as a separate divine being, rather than as a divine concept or avatar of the sun god Ra, is a phenomenon of the early New Kingdom. Thutmose IV evidently saw the Aten as a god in its own right, since "[d]uring his rule an historical text on the underside of a scarab mentions Aten in the vanguard of the pharaoh's army in battle—a role commonly given to Amun."[11] Thutmose's successor, Amenhotep III (Akhenaten's father), seems to have had a personal devotion to the Aten, although he did not neglect the more traditional worship of Amen-Ra. Apparently, Amenhotep III saw no contradictions between his devotion to Amen-Ra and his worship of Aten, since evidence of his reverence for the former

---

Routledge, 2000), 37.
[10] William Kelly Simpson, ed., *The Literature of Ancient Egypt: An Anthology of Stories, Instructions, Stelae, Autobiographies, and Poetry* (New Haven: Yale University Press, 2003), 55. Bracketed insertions are mine.
[11] Hart, *Dictionary*, 38.

includes construction on the great temple of Amen-Ra at Karnak. Evidence of his devotion to the latter includes authorizing construction of a temple to the Aten in Heliopolis (literally "City of the Sun"), taking the name Tekhen-Aten ("Radiance of Aten") as one of his many epithets, and naming his royal barge *Aten-Tjehen* ("Shining Sun Disk").

It was left to Amenhotep III's son Amenhotep IV (later Akhenaten) to take the next steps in the development of the Aten cult. This project began in the fifth year of Amenhotep IV's reign. One of his first steps was to change his name from one meaning "Amen is Pleased" to one meaning "Useful to Aten." That move was highly significant in itself, because it took away the focus on reverence for Amen-Ra as the supreme state god and progenitor of the pharaohs and instead allied the throne with a relatively new deity whose status paled in comparison to that of Amen-Ra, in both political and religious terms.

One of Akhenaten's actions in elevating the cult of the Aten was to move the royal residence from Thebes to a new city called Akhetaten, which means "Horizon of the Aten." Construction of the city began in the fifth year of Akhenaten's reign and was completed a few years later. Akhetaten was located in central Egypt in what is now Amarna, standing about halfway between the ancient city of Thebes to the south and Memphis to the north at the mouth of the Nile Delta. Akhetaten boasted two new temples to the Aten, one small and one large and grand, as well as living quarters for the pharaoh, his family, and his court. Housing was also provided for various nobles, who thought it wise and status-raising to live close to the pharaoh, and for the various administrators and functionaries of both the Egyptian state and the sacred temples to Aten.

Worship of the Aten took place every day. Akhenaten officiated as high priest, although there were other, lesser priests also dedicated to the service of the Aten. On some occasions, Queen Nefertiti and other royal women participated in worship services. Temples to the

Aten were different from those dedicated to other gods in that the Aten's temples had no roofs, in order that the light of the sun might shine into the sanctuary.

By Akhenaten's time, the representation of Aten as having a mixed human-animal form had long been abandoned in favor of a depiction of the sun and its rays, a representation that is, in some ways, more abstract than depictions of other Egyptian deities, since it avoids anthropomorphization in favor of an image of solar—and, hence, divine—power. We see this in one important relief from the Great Temple in Akhetaten, which shows Akhenaten, Nefertiti, and their daughter Meritaten holding up fronds of papyrus while offering worship to the Aten, which is depicted as a disk from which rays pour down onto the pharaoh, his wife, and his child. Some of the rays end in human hands that are poised in a gesture of benediction, while other hands hold ankhs, the Egyptian symbol of life, signifying the lifegiving power of the Aten.

When Akhenaten built his new city and new temples, he intended them to usher in a new era in which the Aten was not only the supreme god but also the only god, who was revered both in itself and in its manifestation in the person of the king. Worship of Amen-Ra was forbidden, as was devotion to Osiris. Temples to the old gods were closed, and their wealth and income were devoted instead to the worship of the Aten. Because of this, Akhenaten is sometimes considered to be an early monotheist, but scholarly opinion is divided over the degree to which Atenism was, in fact, a monotheistic faith.

In addition to building temples and commissioning artworks that showed Akhenaten venerating the Aten, Akhenaten also wrote a hymn to the sun. Hymns to the gods had always been an important part of Egyptian religious practice, so the writing of a hymn was nothing new in itself. What was new, however, is the way that Akhenaten describes the Aten and the believer's relationship to it. Some scholars have compared Akhenaten's hymn to Psalm 104, which similarly praises the God of the Israelites and lists his creative acts. Below are some excerpts from Akhenaten's hymn, side by side with the relevant passages of Psalm 104 from the New International Version:

Akhenaten's Hymn[12]	Psalm 104
You rise in perfection on the horizon of the sky,	The Lord wraps himself in light as with a garment;
living Aten, who determines life.	he stretches out the heavens like a tent
Whenever you are risen upon the eastern horizon	and lays the beams of his upper chambers on their waters.
you fill every land with your perfection.	He makes the clouds his chariot
	and rides on the wings of the wind.
You are appealing, great, sparkling, high over every land;	He makes winds his messengers,
	flames of fire his servants. (vv. 2–4)
your rays embrace the lands as far as everything you have made.	

. . . .

Whenever you set on the western horizon,	He made the moon to mark the seasons,
the land is in darkness in the manner of death.	and the sun knows when to go down.
They sleep in a bedroom with heads under the covers,	You bring darkness, it becomes night,
and one eye cannot see another.	and all the beasts of the forest prowl.

---

[12] Kelly, Literature of Ancient Egypt, 279–80, 283.

. . . .

Every lion comes out of his cave and all the serpents bite,

for darkness is a blanket.

The land is silent now, because He who makes them

is at rest on His horizon.

. . . .

The entire land performs its work:

all the flocks are content with their fodder,

trees and plants grow,

birds fly up to their nests,

their wings extended in praise for your *Ka*.

All the kine prance on their feet;

everything which flies up and alights,

they live when you rise for them.

The barges sail upstream and downstream too,

for every way is open at your rising.

The fishes in the river leap before your face

when your rays are inside the

The lions roar for their prey

and seek their food from God. (vv. 19–21)

How many are your works, Lord!

In wisdom you made them all;

the earth is full of your creatures.

There is the sea, vast and spacious,

teeming with creatures beyond number—

living things both large and small.

There the ships go to and fro,

and Leviathan, which you formed to frolic there.

All creatures look to you

to give them their food at the proper time.

(vv. 24–27)

sea.

. . . .

The earth comes forth into existence by your hand, and you make it.
When you rise, they live; when you set, they die.

. . . .

When you give it to them, they gather it up; when you open your hand, they are satisfied with good things.
When you hide your face, they are terrified; when you take away their breath, they die and return to the dust. (vv. 28-29)

Akhenaten's fervent personal devotion to the Aten was not sufficient to bring about the religious revolution he so desired. Atenism failed to make much headway among the Egyptian populace, who resented the loss of their traditional religion and who were grateful when Akhenaten's heir, Tutankhamen, revived the worship of Amen-Ra, Osiris, and the other gods who had been revered by Egyptians for millennia. During this restoration, the old temples were reopened and the priesthoods restored, and the city of Akhetaten was destroyed by royal command. Akhenaten was treated as a heretic, and his name erased from inscriptions.

Modern opinions of Akhenaten are highly variable. Some authors and scholars have seen him in much the same way as his countrymen apparently did, as a heretic whose religious fervor bordered on mania. Others, however, have seen him as a sincere reformer who wished to replace a polytheistic system with one devoted to a single supreme deity. Those who espouse the latter opinion sometimes try to align Akhenaten's faith with Christianity, attempting to show that Akhenaten was ahead of his time and that his reforms were an improvement. However, most scholars today agree that comparisons of Atenism with other monotheistic religions need to be done carefully in order to avoid both the creation of false parallels between Atenism and other religions and also to steer clear of the assumption that monotheism is somehow superior to other religious expressions.

In addition to receiving significant scholarly attention, Pharaoh Akhenaten has also captured the imagination of modern artists and musicians. One important artwork is the opera *Akhnaten* by the American minimalist composer Philip Glass. *Akhnaten* was written in 1983, and draws its libretto partly from ancient Egyptian texts and partly from a set of letters in Akkadian that were found in the ruins of Akhetaten. Other portions of the libretto are in biblical Hebrew. Each performance of the opera includes a setting of Akhenaten's "Hymn to the Sun," which is always sung in the language of the audience that is watching at the time. The action of the opera starts with the funeral of his father, Amenhotep III. The opera then follows the course of Akhenaten's life, from his coronation to his own death and burial.

The 2016 production by the English National Opera, which was revived in 2018 and 2019, included the Gandini juggling troupe. The troupe's juggling of balls and clubs of various sizes was intended to be symbolic of some of the themes of the opera, and was timed to mesh with and represent the flow of the music.

Atum (Tum, Tem, Atem, Temu)

One of the primary creator gods of ancient Egypt, Atum was said to have emerged on the primeval mound that sat in the primeval waters, which were personified as the god Nun. Atum's name means something like "all" or "complete." His first act of creation was to make Shu, the god of air, and Tefnut, the goddess of light. One version of the story says that Atum made them from his semen, while another says that Shu was made from Atum's spittle and that he vomited Tefnut into existence. From Shu and Tefnut came Geb, the god of the earth, and Nut, the goddess of the sky. Geb and Nut's children were Isis, Osiris, Nephthys, and Set. Together, Atum and his descendants are referred to as the Ennead, the primary deities worshiped in Heliopolis, an ancient city near what is now Cairo. Egyptologist Stephen Quirke notes that before the New Kingdom, Atum and the Ennead were more widely considered to be the primary creator deities throughout Egypt.[13]

Like many other gods, Atum quickly became identified with the sun god Ra, and he was frequently worshiped as Atum-Ra. However, Atum also had his own independent role with respect to solar theology. Ancient Egyptians personified the sun as different deities

---

[13] Stephen Quirke, *Exploring Religion in Ancient Egypt* (Chichester: John Wiley & Sons, 2015), 137.

depending on the time of day. In this system, Atum was the setting sun, while Ra was the sun at midday and Khepera was the rising sun.

The connection between Atum and light is clearly drawn in the myth of the Eye of Ra and the creation of human beings. In this myth, Shu and Tefnut become separated from Atum in the vastness of Nun, so Atum sends his Eye to look for them. While the Eye is away, Atum grows a new one. When the first Eye returns triumphantly with Shu and Tefnut, Atum weeps for joy, and from his tears human beings are created. The first Eye becomes jealous of the second one, so Atum gives the first one pride of place by turning it into the sun disk and putting it on his head.

In addition to his roles as creator and an aspect of the sun, Atum was thought to sometimes take on the form of an ichneumon (Egyptian mongoose). Author Margaret R. Bunson states that this was because of the mongoose's ability to kill venomous serpents without taking harm and because it ate crocodile eggs.[14]

---

[14] Margaret R. Bunson, *Encyclopedia of Ancient Egypt,* rev. ed. (New York: Facts on File, Inc., 2002), 177.

Bastet (Bast, Boubastis, Pasht)

Goddess of fertility and motherhood, protector of the pharaoh, and identified with the Eye of Ra, the cat-headed goddess Bastet originally was conceptualized as a lion-headed deity and often was aligned with Sekhmet, another lion-headed goddess. In fact, Bastet and Sekhmet sometimes were treated as two different facets of the same deity. Because of Bastet's association with Sekhmet, she was also linked with the cow-headed goddess Hathor, who transformed into Sekhmet and destroyed humanity at the command of Ra.

In her cat-headed form, Bastet (also known as Bast) is usually portrayed as having a woman's body, clothed in a linen sheath dress, and carrying a sistrum (a type of rattle) and a box or jar. Both the actual meaning and pronunciation of Bastet's name remain unclear. Egyptologist Geraldine Pinch has suggested that it means something like "She of the Ointment Jar," because Bastet was associated with ointments and perfumes.[15]

Bastet was venerated in her lion form for the first thousand years of Egyptian dynastic history. The shift to her cat form occurred sometime during the second millennium BCE. Pinch notes that the

---

[15] Geraldine Pinch, *A Handbook of Egyptian Mythology* (Santa Barbara: ABC-CLIO, 2002), 115.

different aspects of Bastet "as nurturing mother and terrifying avenger" can be found in many different sources. These include the Pyramid Texts, which date from c. 2400 to 2300 BCE ; the Coffin Texts, which are protective spells written on the insides of coffins, dating from c. 2181 to 2185 BCE; and in the *Book of the Dead,* a New Kingdom funerary text that contains collections of spells and prayers intended to shepherd the soul through the hazards of the Underworld.[16]

Ideas about Bastet's character, as depicted in the myths that involve her, revolved in part around the observed behavior of cats. Bastet was associated with fertility and motherhood because cats themselves are both very fertile and also devoted, attentive mothers. The ferocity of the cat, on the other hand, is shown in a myth in which Bastet helps Ra kill the serpent-demon Apep (also known as Apophis) by attacking it with her claws. The cat's independence and unwillingness to be tamed is reflected in a myth usually referred to as "The Distant Goddess," in which Bastet, in her guise as the Eye of Ra and in feline form, runs away into the desert, and Ra has to send a god (which one varies depending on the version of the story) to coax her to come back home. Geraldine Pinch notes that in Ptolemaic Egypt, the return of the Distant Goddess had importance to the Egyptian calendar and to beliefs about the origin of the Nile floods, since the goddess's return home was said to initiate the inundation of the Nile, which was seen as the beginning of the Egyptian year.[17]

The worship of Bastet was centered in the city of Bubastis, located on the eastern edge of the Nile Delta, where the goddess had a fine temple. The worship of Bastet included votive offerings of bronze cat statuettes and actual mummified cats. The ancient historian Herodotus, who refers to Bastet as the Roman goddess Diana, thought the Temple of Bastet the most beautiful in Egypt.[18] In his

---

[16] Pinch, *Handbook*, 115.
[17] Pinch, *Handbook,* 90.
[18] Herodotus II:137; Henry Cary, trans., *Herodotus* (London: George Bell and Sons, 1901), 150.

description of the temple precincts, Herodotus says that two canals ran from the Nile to the entrance, "one flowing round it on one side, the other on the other," and that trees had been planted along the edges of each canal.[19] In addition, Herodotus says that the temple grounds were surrounded by a wall "sculptured with figures ... and within is a grove of lofty trees, planted round a large temple."[20]

Herodotus also wrote a description of the main festival of Bastet, which historian Lewis Spence says was held in April and May every year.[21] Bastet's festival appears to have been one of the most popular feasts in the Egyptian calendar, drawing up to 700,000 visitors to Bubastis every year, according to Herodotus.[22] This festival was an occasion for great rejoicing, celebrated with sacrifices, processions of barges down the river, music, singing and dancing, and the consumption of enormous amounts of alcohol. Indeed, Herodotus estimated that at the festival of Bastet, "more wine is consumed ... than in all the rest of the year."[23] It is possible that the volume of wine consumed at Bastet's festival was related to the myth of Hathor/Sekhmet, in which the goddess's bloodlust is sated by beer brewed by Ra, which has been colored to look like blood so that Hathor/Sekhmet would drink that rather than the blood of the people. The ruse works; Hathor/Sekhmet drinks until she is senseless, and after that point she has no more desire to kill.

---

[19] Herodotus II:137; Cary, trans., 150.
[20] Herodotus II:137; Cary, trans. 150.
[21] Lewis Spence, *Myths and Legends of Ancient Egypt* (Boston: David D. Nickerson & Co., [1915]), 148.
[22] Herodotus II:60; Cary, trans., 118.
[23] Herodotus II:60; Cary, trans., 118.

The *Book of the Dead* and Other Funerary Texts

Since the Old Kingdom, it had been an Egyptian funerary tradition to write prayers and spells on the walls of the tombs of the pharaohs, to give them the information and power they needed to navigate the dangers of the Tuat and attain eternal life. In the Middle Kingdom, such texts were written inside the coffins of the aristocracy, but during the New Kingdom, collections of prayers and spells began to be produced for any Egyptian person who might have the money to purchase them. These collections, which were written on papyrus scrolls and often illustrated, are referred to as the *Book of the Dead*. The various versions of the *Book of the Dead* constitute some of the most important sources of information about Egyptian myth, cosmology, religion, and funerary practices.

Although these collections are given a single, unitary title, they are far from uniform. Some collections are considerably longer and more lavishly illustrated than others, and it was possible for the person buying one of these books to have them custom-made by selecting which spells and prayers might be included. Other versions of the book seem to have been mass-produced, although the name of the person who bought them could be written inside at the time of purchase.

The *Book of the Dead* was intended to be buried with the deceased so that they could use it to deal with any dangers they might encounter when they arrived in the Tuat. One particularly important section of this book dealt with what one must do during the ceremony of the weighing of the heart, which would determine whether the deceased would be allowed to go on to paradise or whether they would be annihilated forever.

Another funerary text that came into regular use during the New Kingdom was the *Book of the Gates*. The *Book of the Gates* described the twelve sectors of the Underworld and the journey of the sun from west to east during the night, which made it similar to the *Amduat*, another important text. (The *Amduat* is summarized in the chapter on the Tuat below.) The sections of the *Book of the Gates* are aligned with the twelve hours of the night, and each one is populated by different collections of deities and other beings who attempt to either help or hinder Ra on his passage through their territories, a structure shared with the *Amduat*.

Each region of the Tuat in the *Book of the Gates* is described as having a specific gate with its own specific name, and each gate is guarded by a different serpent. For example, the gate of the third hour is named "Mistress of Nurturing," and the guardian serpent is called "the Stinger," while the gate of the seventh hour is called "Gleaming One," and its guardian serpent is called "Hidden Eye."[24]

While the *Book of the Dead* provided protection to the deceased and the *Book of the Gates* explained what the Tuat was like, the *Book of the Opening of the Mouth* contained detailed instructions for the Rite of the Opening of the Mouth, an important funerary liturgy that was performed both on statues and on the mummified remains of deceased persons. Because Egyptian funerary beliefs and

---

[24] Pat Remler, *Egyptian Mythology A to Z*, 3rd ed. (New York: Chelsea House, 2010), 30-31.

practices included offerings of food and drink to the deceased, the Rite of the Opening of the Mouth was vital for allowing the dead person to be able to consume the offerings in the afterlife. Egyptologist Ann Macy Roth has argued that the procedure used in this ritual was intended to mimic

> the birth and maturation of a child. Its purpose was to take the newly reborn deceased person through the transitions of birth and childhood, so that he or she could be nourished by the (adult) food provided in such profusion by Egyptian mortuary cults. The ritual therefore emphasized the aspects of the process that affected the way a child receives nourishment: the initial connection with the placenta, the severing of the umbilical cord, nursing, weaning, and teething.[25]

The rite could have up to seventy-five sections, but less elaborate versions were also performed. Special tools and objects used in the ceremony included incense, ointment, and water, which were all used to purify the statue, and clothing in which the statue was dressed. One particularly important implement was an adze or chisel that was used to ritually "open" the mouth of the statue or the deceased person so that they could breathe, eat, and drink. The *Book of the Dead* refers to this aspect of the ceremony in Chapter 23:

> My mouth is opened by Ptah,
>
> My mouth's bonds are loosed by my city-god.
>
> Thoth has come fully equipped with spells,
>
> He looses the bonds of Seth from my mouth.
>
> Atum has given me my hands,
>
> They are placed as guardians.
>
> My mouth is given to me,

---

[25] Ann Macy Roth, "Fingers, Stars, and the 'Opening of the Mouth': The Nature and Function of the *nṯrwj*-Blades," *The Journal of Egyptian Archaeology* 79 (1993): 60.

My mouth is opened by Ptah

With that chisel of metal

With which he opened the mouth of the gods.[26]

As with other funerary texts, the *Book of the Opening of the Mouth* contains both illustrations and text. However, in the *Book of the Opening of the Mouth*, the illustrations have a different function than those in the *Amduat*, for example. Rather than descriptions of a particular space or collection of deities, the illustrations in the *Book of the Opening of the Mouth* accompany the text explaining how each part of the rite was to be performed. The pictures show who ought to be doing what, as well as how various items such as water were to be utilized.[27]

One interesting aspect of the performance of the Rite of the Opening of the Mouth was the continuum it created between the mortal world and the divine one. Living human priests and their helpers performed the rite on statues and on the mummified bodies of deceased people, but so did funerary gods such as Anubis and Wepwawet, who are sometimes depicted as engaged in actions from the rite. Further, some of the human actors in the rite performed by living priests might take on the role of deities. For example, in the version of the rite preserved in the tomb of pharaoh Seti I, two women participated in the story by representing the goddesses Isis and Nephthys.[28] These human stand-ins for deities, on the one hand, and the pictures of deities performing human actions, on the other, created a complex of links and alignments among myths, religious beliefs, and funerary practices that connected the divine and human worlds, as well as connecting the living and the dead. This is so because the deceased was often thought to become Osiris after death,

---

[26] Miriam Lichtheim, *Ancient Egyptian Literature: A Book of Readings*, Vol. 2: *The New Kingdom* (Berkeley: University of California Press, 1976), 120.

[27] A complete edition of the book as it exists in the tomb of Seti I is E. A. Wallace Budge, *The Book of Opening the Mouth: The Egyptian Texts With English Translations* (London: Kegan Paul, Trench, Trübner & Co., Ltd., 1909), 2 vols.

[28] Budge, Opening the Mouth I, 12.

so as to enter into everlasting life, and since Osiris was mourned by Isis and Nephthys after he was murdered by Set, so too did the deceased person require someone to represent these goddesses so that they might be properly mourned just as Osiris was.

The Four Sons of Horus

The sons of Horus the Elder had several roles within Egyptian religious and cosmological belief. In terms of cosmology, they were thought to be the four pillars that held up the sky, and they were often associated with the four cardinal directions. However, the greater part of their function was in relation to funerary practices, since they were thought to assist the transit of the soul into the afterlife. They are often depicted in funerary papyri, and in the Pyramid Texts, they are called upon to protect and guide the soul of the pharaoh as it enters the afterlife. Sculpted heads of the sons of Horus sometimes were used as guardians of the canopic jars used in mummification.

Ancient Egyptian burial practices involved the careful removal of the internal organs preparatory to embalming the body. The stomach, intestines, lungs, and liver were each placed in their own special jars, sometimes known as "canopic jars." These organs were carefully preserved and buried with the rest of the body, since the ancient Egyptians believed that the organs would be reunited with the body in the afterlife. (The heart was left inside the body so that it could be used in the ceremony of the weighing of the heart.)

The style of the lids for the canopic jars underwent changes as time passed. The oldest jars have plain lids, while those from the First

Intermediate Period are decorated with human heads. During the New Kingdom, the style changed yet again, with each lid being fashioned to represent one of the four sons of Horus the Elder. Each of these gods was associated with a specific protector goddess, and each had a specific role as a guardian of one of the preserved organs.

Duamutef

Duamutef had the head of a jackal. He was the guardian of the stomach, and was associated with the east. His guardian goddess was Neith.

Hapy (1; also Hapi)

Hapy had the head of a baboon and protected the lungs. He was associated with the north, and his guardian goddess was Nephthys. (For the deity of the same name who was associated with the Nile floods, see Hapy (2) below).

Imsety (Imset, Imseti, Amset, Amsety, Mesti, Mesta)

Associated with the south, Imsety had human form and protected the liver. His guardian goddess was Isis.

Qebehsenuef (Qebhsenuf)

Qebehsenuef's guardian was Serket, a goddess of fertility and healing, who was especially associated with protection against venomous stings and bites. Qebehsenuef was depicted as having a hawk's head. He was associated with the east and protected the intestines.

Geb (Seb, Keb, Kebb, Gebb)

The offspring of Shu and Tefnut, Geb was the god of earth, and his consort was the sky goddess Nut. Geb was part of the Ennead (Nine Gods) of the city of Heliopolis, a group of deities that included Geb's father, wife, and children. In visual representations, Geb is often depicted together with Shu and Nut. In these images, Geb lies on the ground, while Nut arches her body over him, with only her fingers and toes touching him at the ends of his body. Meanwhile, Shu stands in the middle of Geb's body, where he holds Nut up with his arms. This represents the sky arching over the earth, with air both separating the earth from the sky and also keeping the sky in position.

Like Osiris, Geb was sometimes depicted in myth as a pseudo-historical king of Egypt. However, unlike Osiris, who is a just and gentle god, Geb is ruthless, jealous, and violent. In a myth from the Thirtieth Dynasty that is preserved in a shrine in Phakussa (now Faqus) on the eastern edge of the Nile Delta, Geb's father Shu holds the throne of Egypt, and has ruled for a very long time. Geb is jealous of his father's power and is still angry that Shu separated him from his beloved wife, Nut. Geb leads a revolt that ousts Shu, after which Geb rapes his mother, Tefnut. Nine days of howling winds and violent storms follow Geb's actions, but when everything dies down, Geb takes the throne and is acknowledged as the king. When Geb attempts to take his father's crown, the *uraeus*, or cobra, that adorns it spits out venom that burns Geb and kills his followers. Geb is healed by a lock of Ra's hair, and he eventually settles down to become a good ruler. When Geb decides to abdicate, he designates Horus as his heir in the north and Set as his heir in the south.

Geb was also sometimes identified as the "Great Cackler," the goose that laid the primordial egg from which the universe emerged. He is therefore sometimes depicted with a goose's head. At other times, he is rendered as a human king, wearing the combined crown of both Upper and Lower Egypt.

Hapy (2; also Hapi)

Associated with the yearly flooding of the Nile, Hapy was one of the most revered gods in the Egyptian pantheon. Hapy was said to live variously in the Underworld or on an island in Elephantine in the First Cataract of the Nile. On the island, Hapy resided in a grotto that was guarded by the god Khnum.

Hapy wears a man's kilt and a headdress of papyrus plants. He is usually represented as an intersex figure, having the beard and hair of a male but the breasts of a female. He also usually has a pot belly. Hapy is portrayed with breasts and a belly because he was considered to be a nurturing, nourishing figure, since life in ancient Egypt was completely dependent on the fecundity brought by the annual floods. Hapy often has blue or green skin, and in the New Kingdom he was sometimes portrayed as a pair of identical gods pulling on the stems of two plants that are entwined together. In this form, Hapy represents the union of Upper and Lower Egypt.

Hapy was intimately linked with Osiris in the Egyptian religious imagination. Just as Osiris returned to life after being dead, Hapy revived Egypt every year with life-giving floodwaters. Osiris was considered to be the god who first taught people how to grow and harvest grain, and since Hapy's floods made agriculture possible, the return of the crops every year was thought to symbolize the resurrection of Osiris. The harvest that followed the floods therefore was both a commemoration and renewal of Osiris's gifts of barley and agriculture.[29]

A surviving hymn to Hapy praises him for his bounty, and it is clear from the text that the time of the Nile floods was an occasion for celebration in ancient Egypt. The hymn also makes clear that inundations that were insufficient or overwhelming might spell disaster, and so Hapy might have a destructive aspect as well as a nurturing one. Below are some excerpts from this hymn, which dates from the Middle Kingdom:[30]

> Hail to you, Hapy,
>
> Sprung from earth,
>
> Come to nourish Egypt!
>
> Of secret ways,
>
> A darkness by day,
>
> To whom his followers sing!
>
> . . . .
>
> When he is sluggish, noses clog,
>
> Everyone is poor;
>
> As the sacred loaves are pared,
>
> A million perish among men.
>
> When he plunders, the whole land rages,
>
> Great and small roar;
>
> People change according to his coming,
>
> When Khnum has fashioned him.
>
> . . . .

---

[29] Pinch, *Handbook*, 137.

[30] Miriam Lichtheim, *Ancient Egyptian Literature: A Book of Readings*, Vol. 1: *The Old and Middle Kingdoms* (Berkeley: University of California Press, 1973), 205–09.

When he rises at the residence,

Men feast on the meadows' gifts,

Decked with lotus for the nose,

And all the things that sprout from the earth.

Children's hands are filled with herbs,

They forget to eat.

Good things are strewn about the houses,

The whole land leaps for joy.

. . . .

Oh joy when you come!

You who feed men and herds

With your meadow gifts!

Oh joy when you come!

Hathor

Hathor is a complex deity who played multiple important roles within Egyptian religion and culture. She was seen as a nurturing cow-goddess, a patron of fertility and motherhood. Hathor also had strong associations with music, dance, drunkenness, and sensuality. As one of the goddesses who represented the Eye of Ra, Hathor had a terrifying, destructive aspect as well. This dual nature as nurturing cow and fierce Eye of Ra is often captured in representations of the goddess, where she is shown as a beautiful woman wearing a headdress of two long, curving cow horns between which is set the sun disk.

Whether Hathor was worshiped in the Predynastic Period is still an open question. Egyptologist Carolyn Graves-Brown notes that "[t]he first clear attestation of Hathor is in the reign of Khafre in the Fourth Dynasty."[31] Once the cult of Hathor became established, however, it became immensely popular. Hathor's primary cult center was at Dendera in central Egypt, but Graves-Brown says that "more temples were built to [Hathor] than to any other Egyptian goddess."[32]

---

[31] Carolyn Graves-Brown, *Dancing for Hathor: Women in Ancient Egypt* (London: Continuum, 2010), 17.
[32] Graves-Brown, *Dancing for Hathor*, xi.

In addition to serving as the Eye of Ra, Hathor was sometimes considered to be Ra's mother and therefore the mother of the pharaoh by extension. This connection was reinforced by images that showed Hathor nursing the pharaoh.[33] The living pharaoh participated in a rite intended to represent him nursing at Hathor's breast. In this rite, the pharaoh would drink from the teats of sacred cows that were kept at the Temple of Hathor. Geraldine Pinch notes that this activity "was part of the coronation ceremony, and seems to have been regularly repeated."[34]

Hathor's motherly role extended beyond the boundaries of life. She was one of the goddesses said to live in the Field of Reeds, which was the Egyptian name for paradise. Just as men were thought to take the name of Osiris upon death, so too did women take the name of Hathor, although the latter was a relatively late development.[35] As a goddess of death, Hathor's duty was to shepherd the soul into the afterlife and see to the soul's comfort. We see this in one prayer found on a cup dating from c. 1550 BCE, where one of the well-wishes for the dead person is "[m]ay Hathor give you beer."[36]

It is Hathor who gives the soul beer because of the goddess's role in the myth of the destruction of humanity. In the myth, Ra is angry because human beings are doing evil things and neglecting the worship of the gods. Ra sends Hathor down to Earth as his Eye to wreak destruction and teach the humans a lesson. Unfortunately, Hathor becomes so wrapped up in this task that she risks destroying all humanity, so the other gods beg Ra to restrain her, otherwise no one will be left to worship them. Ra achieves this by having beer brewed and then colored red. Hathor, who has taken on the guise of

---

[33] Margaret Bunson, *Encyclopedia of Ancient Egypt*, rev. ed. (New York: Facts on File, Inc., 2002), 160.

[34] Geraldine Pinch, *Magic in Ancient Egypt* (London: British Museum Press, 1994), 83.

[35] Mark Smith, Following Osiris: Perspectives on the Osirian Afterlife from Four Millennia (Oxford: Oxford University Press, 2017), 252, 417.

[36] Stephen Quirke, *Exploring Religion in Ancient Egypt* (Chichester: John Wiley & Sons Ltd., 2010), 69.

the lion-headed goddess Sekhmet, thinks the beer is blood, and she drinks so deeply of it that she passes out drunk. When she wakes up, she is once again restored to her senses.

Beer, drinking, and drunkenness were essential parts of Hathor's feasts. These festivals were also occasions for the expression of joy through music and dance. Hathor was especially associated with the sound of the sistrum, a kind of metallic rattle, and while dance was part of the worship of many Egyptian gods, it was especially connected with Hathor. Graves-Brown notes that dance was sufficiently important to the worship of Hathor that men sometimes danced as well. And not only that, but there were times when the pharaoh himself danced for the goddess.[37]

One aspect of Hathor had particular duties regarding newborn children. This form of Hathor divided her into seven goddesses, and in this form, she visited newborn children and declared what their fates would be. The Seven Hathors could also be called upon in matters of love and were thought to offer protection against demons.[38]

Hathor also participated in the Osiris legend that was central to many Egyptian religious practices. Some scholars think that an older version of the myth cast Hathor in the role of wife to Osiris and mother to Horus, a role that was later taken over by Isis.[39] Hathor plays a different role in a continuation of the Osiris legend known as "The Battle of Horus and Set," wherein the young Horus has to defend his claim to the throne against his evil uncle, the chaos god Set. In this story, Ra and the other gods act as judges who are attempting to figure out whether to grant the crown to Horus or Set. At one point, Ra gets so fed up with the proceedings that he goes into his tent by himself to sulk. The other gods discuss what might be done to alleviate Ra's foul mood, and Hathor volunteers to deal with the problem. She goes into Ra's tent, where she takes off her clothes.

---

[37] Graves-Brown, *Dancing for Hathor*, xi.
[38] Pinch, Magic in Ancient Egypt, 37, 81.
[39] See, for example, Hart, *Dictionary*, 62.

When Ra sees Hathor's naked body, his good mood is restored, and he returns to his rightful place among the gods.

Hathor's association with Horus continued even after Isis supplanted Hathor as his mother. In some places, Hathor was considered to be the consort of Horus. This was true particularly in Edfu, where a fine temple to Horus was built during the Ptolemaic Period. Egyptologist Rosalie David notes that one annual event at the temple in Edfu involved taking the statue of Hathor from her temple in Dendera and sailing it down the river to Edfu, where ceremonies would be held celebrating the marriage of Hathor and Horus.[40] When the festival was over, the statue would then be sailed back to Dendera and returned to its shrine.

---

[40] A. Rosalie David, *Discovering Ancient Egypt* (New York: Facts on File, 1994), 38.

Horus (Hor, Her, Heru, Har)

Horus is one of the oldest and most complex deities in the Egyptian pantheon and perhaps is one of the most familiar to modern readers. Horus is usually pictured as a falcon, or else as a man with a falcon's head. In either depiction, he is sometimes seen wearing the *pschent* crown of a united Upper and Lower Egypt. At other times, he is shown as a young, winged human boy with his finger raised to his lips; this version of the god was taken up by the Greeks as Harpocrates, the god of the keeping of secrets.

From the beginning of Egyptian history, Horus was a god allied with kingship. The Pre-Dynastic pharaoh Menes, who united Upper and Lower Egypt into a single country, was especially devoted to Horus, which helped to nationalize Horus's cult. However, it was not merely that the king worshiped Horus fervently that united the god with the throne. One primary tenet of Egyptian kingship was that the king himself was a god, and that he specifically was a manifestation or even reincarnation of Horus. This link was cemented when, upon assuming the throne, the king took a new name that was referred to as his "Horus name."

Understanding the nature of Horus is made difficult by the multiplicity of his manifestations. It is unclear whether these were intended to be avatars of the same deity, or whether they were, in fact, separate gods entirely. One version of Horus, often referred to as "Horus the Elder," was said to be the child of the earth god Geb and the sky goddess Nut, making him the brother of Isis, Osiris, Nephthys, and Set. The second version is usually called "Horus the Younger," and in this manifestation, he is the child of Isis and Osiris.

From the earliest times, Horus the Elder was a sky god, whose eyes were the sun and moon. The antiquity of this association with the sky is noted by Egyptologist Geraldine Pinch, who observes that "[o]ne of the earliest divine images known from Egypt is that of a falcon in a barque,"[41] a common ancient Egyptian depiction of the movement of a heavenly body across the sky, which was conceived of as a kind of celestial waterway. In later times, Horus became identified with the sun god Ra, thus assuming a solar aspect himself. Pinch explains that in this manifestation, he was known as "Ra-Horakhty (Ra-Horus of the Double Horizon), who triumphed over his enemies to rise in the east."[42]

Horus the Younger was said to be the child of Isis and Osiris, who was conceived after his father's death through a magical act performed by his mother. In the Osirian myth, Horus is in constant danger from his evil uncle Set, who kills Horus's father not once but twice in an effort to usurp his throne. The manifestation of Horus as the son of Isis and Osiris was commonly co-opted by Egyptian pharaohs at least by the Fifth Dynasty. These pharaohs considered themselves to be both the descendants of Horus and a reincarnation thereof. This association is asserted in the Pyramid Texts, which refer to the pharaoh as Horus when he is a living man and as Osiris once he has died and entered the afterlife.

In addition to the Osirian tale, the other primary myth involving Horus is "The Battle of Horus and Set," a story preserved in a papyrus dating from the Twentieth Dynasty. In this tale, Set has usurped the throne of Egypt after the death of Osiris. Horus comes

---

[41] Pinch, *Handbook*, 143.
[42] Pinch, *Handbook*, 144.

before the supreme god Ra-Horakhty and all the other gods to demand that he be named Osiris's rightful heir. The gods argue back and forth about this. Most of them agree that Horus should be king, but Ra-Horakhty and a few others think that Set should retain the throne because he is older and more experienced. The gods ask for advice from Osiris and from the goddess Neith, both of whom say that Horus should wear the crown.

When the court of the gods fails to reach a consensus, Set suggests a single combat between himself and Horus, with the victor being made king. In the first combat, Set and Horus turn themselves into hippopotamuses to see who can remain under water the longest. Horus's mother Isis tries to rig the contest by harpooning Set, but her first cast goes awry, hitting Horus instead. The second cast hits Set, who rages at his sister for harming him. Isis feels sorry for Set, and so she removes the harpoon, but this angers Horus, who attacks his mother and cuts off her head. Horus then runs off into the mountains with Isis's head, while her body becomes a headless statue. (Later in the story, Isis revives herself.)

Ra-Horakhty demands that Horus pay for his crime, so he sends various gods out to find him. Set comes across Horus while he is sleeping and gouges out his eyes, then denies having seen Horus at all. Horus is later found by Hathor, who heals him and brings him back home. At this point, Ra-Horakhty is so fed up with both Set and Horus that he tells them to go home, eat together, and stop fighting each other.

Set invites Horus home to have a meal with him and to be his guest overnight. Horus agrees, but once he is asleep, Set attempts to rape him. Horus manages to fend Set off, but not before Set has ejaculated into his hands. Later, Set tries to convince the gods that Horus wanted Set to have sex with him and that therefore he is unclean. However, Set is the one who ends up being shamed when his semen calls out to the court of the gods from the river, where Isis had cast Horus's befouled hands (she makes him new ones afterward), and from inside Set's own body, since he had eaten lettuce upon which Isis had secretly poured some of his seed.

Set then proposes another contest. He and Horus are to make boats of stone. Whichever one makes a stone boat that floats on the water gets to be king. Horus cheats by making a boat of plaster and wood that looks like stone, and so wins the contest, upon which Set turns himself into a hippopotamus and rips Horus's boat to shreds.

The suit between Horus and Set is finally decided when Osiris sends one last letter saying that he will harvest the hearts of those who refuse to deal justly with their fellows. This frightens the gods into making a final decision. Set is bound in chains and Horus is made king, at which point Set concedes the throne to him, and the gods rejoice that the issue has finally been decided.

Imhotep (Imouthes)

Deification of rulers, whether during their lifetimes or shortly after their deaths, was a common occurrence in the ancient world. Egyptian kings were thought to be both the offspring and living manifestation of a god, usually Horus or Amen-Ra. It was rather less common for other persons to achieve deified status, although it did happen from time to time. For ancient Egypt, we see this particularly in the person of Imhotep, the vizier of the First Dynasty pharaoh Djoser and probable architect of Djoser's step pyramid in what is now Saqqara. Imhotep eventually was worshiped as a god of wisdom and healing.

Imhotep's glorification and later deification grew out of a tradition of reverence for his wisdom and skill, because the historical Imhotep was a talented, skilled man who was more than worthy of the pharaoh's trust. Over time, Imhotep's legend acquired various accretions. Through these accretions, Imhotep eventually was credited with the authorship of several wisdom texts, was supposed to have been a physician and healer, and was eventually considered to be the son of Ptah, the supreme god of Memphis. Some versions of Imhotep's parentage state that his mother, Khereduankh, was a mortal woman, while others claimed she was the daughter of the god Banebdjedet, which led some people to revere her as a divine being in her own right. A third claim about Imhotep's origins makes him fully divine, stating that he was the son of Ptah and Sekhmet. Alignment of Imhotep with Ptah, rather than with a different deity, stems from Ptah's role as the patron of architects, builders, and craftsmen. In his role as a wise man, Imhotep also became a patron god of scribes.

Accretions to Imhotep's legend and his eventual deification occurred over a very long span of time. References to Imhotep as a glorified or deified figure only appear beginning in the Middle Kingdom, hundreds of years after Imhotep's death. Moreover, legends about Imhotep and various facets of his biography seem to have been created out of whole cloth; there is no evidence that he himself wrote wisdom texts (although one attributed to him does survive) or served as a healer, and his supposed divine or semi-divine status obviously is a work of imagination rather than fact.

One early posthumous reference to Imhotep comes from one of the Harper's Songs. The texts of these songs are sometimes found inscribed in tombs and sometimes on papyrus scrolls. The text of the song in question is preserved in a New Kingdom papyrus, but the language dates it to the Middle Kingdom.[43] In the papyrus, the song is labeled as having been found in the tomb of King Intef, but since several kings used that name, it is impossible to know exactly which one is intended by the label. The song is a meditation on death; below is a brief excerpt:

> Yet those who built tombs,
>
> Their places are gone,
>
> What has become of them?
>
> I have heard the words of Imhotep and Hardedef,
>
> Whose sayings are recited whole.
>
> What of their places?

---

[43] Lichtheim, *Literature* 1, 195

Their walls have crumbled,

Their places are gone,

As though they had never been![44]

In this song, we can see that Imhotep is revered but not yet considered a divine being, since the song claims that he is dead.

At least by the reign of Amenhotep III, however, Imhotep was receiving worship in the form of libations. The text of a libation prayer is attested in multiple papyri up through the Late Period.[45] Further, it is during the Late Period that Imhotep begins to be seen as a divine being, and by the Ptolemaic Period his godhood seems to have been well established.[46] During the Ptolemaic Period, Imhotep became quite popular among the Greeks, who identified Imhotep with Asclepius, the Greek god of physicians and healing.

Two legends survive that recall Imhotep's deeds. One is a Ptolemaic-era stele that preserves the legend of King Djoser and the famine, which is summarized in the chapter on the god Khnum below. The other tale is much later, having been preserved on a Roman-period papyrus from the Tebtunis Temple Library. Below is a summary of the Tebtunis story by archaeologist Marina Escolano-Poveda:

> This text and other sources describe [Imhotep's] divine father Ptah, his mother Khereduankh, and his sister Renpetneferet, sometimes also referred to as his wife. Imhotep is depicted as a powerful magician in Djoser's royal court. In one episode, he travels to Assyria to recover the 42

---

[44] Lichtheim, *Literature* 1, 196. Hardedef was another wise man from the Old Kingdom who was deified.

[45] Dietrich Wildung, *Egyptian Saints: Deification in Pharaonic Egypt* (New York: New York University Press, 1977), 34.

[46] Pinch, *Handbook*, 148

limbs of Osiris and fights in a magical
contest against an Assyrian sorceress.[47]

In addition to the magical powers attributed to the living Imhotep in the Tebtunis story, other late texts also ascribe to him divine powers after his death and elevation to godhood. A stele carved during the reign of Cleopatra VII was made in memory of Taimhotep, wife of the high priest of Ptah at Memphis. Part of the stele is devoted to the story of how Taimhotep was finally able to give her husband a male heir, which she achieved after she and her husband prayed together to Imhotep, "the god great in wonders, effective in deeds, who gives a son to him who has none."[48] That the cult of Imhotep was both popular and important is also shown by the preservation of a hymn addressed to him in the Temple of Ptah at Karnak, which was located next to the great temple to Amen-Ra, one of the most important religious centers in all of ancient Egypt.

---

[47] Marina Escolano-Poveda, "Imhotep: A Sage Between Fiction and Reality," American Research Center in Egypt website, accessed 23 June 2020, https://www.arce.org/resource/imhotep-sage-between-fiction-and-reality.
[48] Miriam Lichtheim, *Ancient Egyptian Literature: A Book of Readings*, Vol. 3: *The Late Period* (Berkeley: University of California Press, 1980), 62.

Isis

The goddess Isis is one of the Egyptian deities most familiar to people today. Originally a goddess of fertility, motherhood, and childbirth, Isis was also considered to be an ancestor of the pharaohs of Egypt, who were thought to be both the direct descendants of Isis's son, Horus, and manifestations of Horus himself. Isis was associated with magic and with healing, and many surviving prayers and magic spells call upon her for aid. Isis appears to have been a relatively obscure goddess in the Early Dynastic Period (also known as the Archaic Period), which began c. 3100 BCE, but she became one of the most important and enduring figures of the Egyptian pantheon. After the conquest of Egypt by Alexander the Great, the Greeks and Romans also began to worship Isis, constructing their own rites and mysteries around her cult. Even today, some modern pagans worship Isis and create rituals around her myth.

The earliest apparent reference to Isis may be on a tablet made by Hor-Aha, an early First Dynasty pharaoh of the Archaic Period. This tablet refers to "Sothis, Opener of the Year, Inundation 1," which might be a reference to Isis because she was often linked with Sothis, the star that we know today as Sirius, whose rising always signaled the flooding of the Nile, an event that was vital to ancient Egyptian agriculture.[49]

Otherwise, the first written references to Isis date from the next major period in ancient Egyptian history, the Old Kingdom, and more specifically from the Fifth Dynasty. These references appear in writings known collectively as the Pyramid Texts, which are inscriptions on the walls of the tombs of some of the pharaohs of Egypt and their queens in what is now Saqqara, Egypt, which originally had been the Egyptian capital of Memphis. The earliest Pyramid Texts are in the tomb of Unas, who ruled Egypt between c. 2375 and c. 2345 BCE. However, Egyptologist James P. Allen states that the somewhat archaic form of the language used for the texts in Unas's tomb suggests that they may in fact be much older.[50]

In all of the Pyramid Texts, Isis functions as one of the deities who cares for the soul of the pharaoh as it makes its transition into the afterlife. For example, texts in the pyramid of Unas depict Isis offering her breast for the soul of Unas to suckle and asking her to bring him back to life, just as she did for her husband/brother, Osiris.[51] Isis also performs similar services for the other kings and queens whose tombs preserve these texts, most of which date from the Sixth Dynasty, although one dates from the Eighth.

Egyptologist Susan Tower Hollis observes parallels between Isis's role as a guide into the afterlife with the role of human women who prepared the bodies for burial. Like human women, Isis is not alone in her task; in the Pyramid Texts she is consistently paired with her sister, Nephthys.[52] Hollis notes further that the familiar story of

---

[49] Normandi Ellis, Feasts of Light: Celebrations for the Seasons of Life Based on the Egyptian Goddess Mysteries (Wheaton: The Theosophical Publishing House, 1999), 3.

[50] Allen, *Pyramid Texts*, 4.

[51] Allen, *Pyramid Texts*, 20, 35.

[52] Susan Tower Hollis, *Five Egyptian Goddesses: Their Possible Beginnings, Actions, and Relationships in the Third Millennium BCE* (n.c.: Bloomsbury Publishing, 2019), n.p. Accessed on Google Books, http://www.google.com/books.

Osiris's death and Isis's subsequent search for and resurrection of his body is primarily retained not in ancient Egyptian sources but in the works of the Roman historian and scholar Plutarch, whose *De Iside et Osiride* ("Concerning Isis and Osiris") was written in the second century CE.[53]

Isis's connection to Egyptian royal authority is attested in part by the use of a throne as a sort of headdress in many ancient Egyptian visual representations of the goddess. Indeed, her name in Egyptian is *Eset,* which literally means "seat" or "throne." However, this is not the only way in which Isis is depicted. During the New Kingdom, Isis begins to be shown wearing a crown of cow's horns that hold up a sun disk, attesting to the conflation of Isis with the cow-goddess Hathor, an earlier Egyptian goddess whose popularity waned as that of Isis grew.

Although Isis was hailed as a goddess of fertility, especially with reference to the annual flooding of the Nile that brought in the rich silt that made farming possible in Egypt's arid desert climate, she was not herself a creator goddess but rather the great-great-granddaughter of the original creator god, Atum.

According to the myth of Isis and Osiris, Osiris becomes the ruler of Egypt, teaching people agriculture and law. When Seth becomes jealous of Osiris's power, he creates a chest made precisely to Osiris's measurements. Seth tricks Osiris into getting into the chest and then dumps it into the Nile, where it floats all the way to the Delta. When the chest washes up on the shore, a tamarisk tree grows around it. The tree is later felled by the king of Byblos, who uses it in the construction of his house.

Distraught at Osiris's disappearance, Isis goes searching for him. She eventually locates the tree—now being used as a pillar—and manages to free Osiris from it. By this time, Osiris is dead, so Isis carries his body to a swamp, where she hides from the vengeful Seth.

---

[53] Hollis, Five Egyptian Goddesses, n.p.

Seth eventually finds the hiding place while Isis is away and dismembers Osiris's body, scattering the pieces throughout the land.

Once again, Isis goes looking for her husband, this time with the help of her sister, Nephthys. The sisters manage to find and reconnect all the parts of Osiris's body except his penis, which has landed in the Nile and has been eaten by a fish. Osiris comes back to life through the force of Isis's magic, but because his body is incomplete, he can no longer stay among the living; he has become a mummy, and thus he passes into the Underworld to become the lord of the dead. Isis then gives birth to Horus, the son Osiris gives her when she magically removes his seed from him while she is in the form of a kite, a small bird of prey.

In this myth, we can see many connections between Isis and various aspects of Egyptian life and religion. The myth designates her as the originator of mummification and a participant in funerary rites along with her sister, Nephthys; her magic allows the dead to return to life and to move into the Underworld, a role that she is repeatedly called upon to play in funerary writings such as the Pyramid Texts; and she becomes the mother of the royal houses of Egypt through her son, Horus.

For all her importance to Egyptian religion and funerary practices, Isis did not have a temple of her own until fairly late, and even then, most of those temples were built by rulers who were not themselves Egyptians. The earliest temple to Isis was erected c. 690 BCE by the Cushite pharaoh Taharqa in Philae, an important sacred center near the First Cataract of the Nile. The temple at Philae was enlarged by Nectanebo II, the last Egyptian pharaoh, in the mid-fourth century BCE, but otherwise the rest of the construction was overseen by non-Egyptians, including some of the Hellenistic rulers during the Ptolemaic Period and then later by the Roman emperors Augustus, Tiberius, and Hadrian.

The temple complex at Philae remained in use for the worship of Isis until the middle of the sixth century CE, when it was converted into a Christian church by Byzantine Emperor Justinian I (527–565 CE). In modern times, the temple complex was removed to an island in the middle of Lake Nasser because of damage from the flooding caused by the Aswan Dam. The temple underwent heavy restoration work as part of the moving process, and was reopened to the public in 1980.

The end of nearly three thousand years of Egyptian dynastic rule, beginning with the Persian conquest in 343 BCE, had important effects on Egyptian religious practices. A succession of Persian kings held sway over Egypt until 332 BCE, when the Macedonian military leader Alexander the Great swooped in and took over the country. Alexander's conquest set in motion the Hellenization of Egypt, a process that gained steam after 309 BCE, when the Macedonian Argead succession came to an abrupt end with the assassination of Alexander's son. After a brief interregnum, a Greek companion of Alexander's took the throne of Egypt as Ptolemy I Soter ("Ptolemy the Savior") in 305 BCE.

Ptolemy's accession ushered in a period of alteration of Egyptian culture through the importation of Greek rulers and Greek immigrants. This influx of Greek culture influenced certain aspects of Egyptian culture and religious practices, despite the support of the Ptolemaic rulers for native Egyptian religious expression, and despite Egyptian resentment toward their Greek overlords. The Roman conquest of Egypt in 30 BCE created additional ties between Egypt and the Roman Empire, ensuring interplay between Roman and Egyptian culture as well.

One outcome of this exchange among Egyptian, Greek, and Roman cultures was the growth of the Isis cult, which found sturdy footholds in both Greece and Rome, although acceptance of the worship of Egyptian deities in Rome initially met with some official governmental resistance.[54] Alexander's capital city of Alexandria,

---

[54] Herwig Maehler, "Roman Poets on Egypt," in *Ancient Perspectives on Egypt*, ed. by Roger Matthews and Cornelia Roemer (London: UCL Press, 2003), 205.

situated on Egypt's Mediterranean coast along the northwestern edge of the Nile Delta, was a prominent locus for the growth of this cult. Alexandria's strategic location, economic power, and reputation as a seat of learning made it an ideal place for people from Greece and other parts of the ancient world to do business and to start new lives, and part of that process was the adoption and transformation of local religious ideas and practices.

However, the Hellenic expansion of the Isis cult was not entirely organic. Ptolemy I recognized the need to integrate Greek and Egyptian religious practices, and so he commanded two priests, Manetho, a native Egyptian, and Timotheus, the son of Greek immigrants, to help align the two religions and smooth over the places where important conceptions about the various deities were in conflict.[55] Historian R. E. Witt reports that the result of Manetho and Timotheus's collaboration was the elevation of Isis and her son Horus to the status of Alexandria's primary deities, with Anubis following close behind. But a mother goddess is nothing without a consort, so a new deity named Serapis (or Sarapis) was created, both as an outgrowth of the cult of the Apis bull at Memphis and as a syncretization of aspects of Greek deities, such as Zeus and Hades, with aspects of Egyptian deities, such as Osiris and Amen.[56]

Isis herself underwent a process of syncretization. Ancient Greek writers such as Diodorus Siculus and Herodotus identified her with Demeter, while Plutarch aligned her with Demeter's daughter, Persephone.[57] Historian Vincent Arieh Tobin states that the identification of Isis with Demeter has to do in part with the roles of both Demeter and Isis as goddesses of fertility and, in particular, with their association with grain crops, while author Joshua J. Mark

---

[55] R. E. Witt, *Isis in the Ancient World* (Baltimore: Johns Hopkins University Press, 1971), 52.
[56] Witt, Isis in the Ancient World, 52–53.
[57] Vincent Arieh Tobin, "Isis and Demeter: Symbols of Divine Motherhood," *Journal of the American Research Center in Egypt* 28 (1991): 187–8.

suggests that it is the journey of each goddess to find a deceased loved one that linked the two in the minds of ancient Greeks.[58]

However the goddess Isis was perceived by worshipers or her identity shaped for public perception by rulers, it is undeniable that her cult became one of the most important in many locations throughout the Mediterranean Basin during the Ptolemaic Period. We can see her importance in the Isis aretalogy, or list of deeds, from Cyme in Asia Minor, which was probably written sometime in the second century CE by a Greek named Demetrius, who claimed to have copied it from a stele at the temple of Hephaestus in Memphis. In the excerpt from the aretalogy given below, Isis claims to be the daughter of the Greek god Kronos and is elevated to the status of a creator goddess as well as an establisher of order and ruler over various aspects of nature:

> I gave and ordained laws for men, which no one is able to change.
>
> I am eldest daughter of Kronos.
>
> I am wife and sister of King Osiris.
>
> I am she who findeth fruit for men.
>
> I am mother of King Horus.
>
> I am she that riseth in the Dog Star
>
> For me was the city of Bubastis built.
>
> I divided the earth from the heaven.
>
> I showed the paths of the stars.
>
> I ordered the course of the sun and the moon.
>
> I devised business in the sea.[59]

[58] Tobin, "Isis and Demeter," 188; Joshua J. Mark, "Isis," *Ancient History Encyclopedia*,19 February 2016, https://www.ancient.eu/isis/.

[59] Reprinted in Marvin W. Meyer, ed., *The Ancient Mysteries: A Sourcebook* (San Francisco: Harper & Row, 1987), 173.

In addition to syncretizing Egyptian and Greek deities, Hellenized worship of Isis, along with its eventual Roman expression, took the form of a mystery cult similar to the Eleusinian Mysteries, which were celebrated in honor of the Greek goddess Demeter. Mystery cults had extensive rules for how one might become an initiate and complex rituals that guided the practice of initiation and worship. Information about the shape of the mysteries of Isis survives in the *Metamorphoses* by Apuleius, a Numidian writing in Latin in the second century CE. Apuleius's *Metamorphoses* is also known as *The Golden Ass*, after the central misfortune of the protagonist, Lucius, who is turned into a donkey. Lucius is later restored to his human form by the goddess Isis, whereupon he becomes an initiate in the mysteries of that goddess. Historian Antonía Tripolitis provides this summary of the mysteries according to Apuleius:

> [I]nitiation into the Isaic cult was limited to individuals who were selected by Isis herself and who were able to afford the high expenses involved in the initiation. These individuals were notified of the honor by Isis in a dream. Prior to the initiation, the individual underwent a bath of purification and 10 days of strict fasting. The initiate was then dressed in a linen robe and permitted to enter the sanctuary where he/she wandered in the dark places of the underworld and underwent certain trials. The morning after the initiation, the initiate, standing on a wooden podium before the statue of Isis, was presented to the crowd. This day was considered a new birthday for the initiate. It signified that he/she had

> died to the old life and was reborn to a
> new course of life and salvation under
> the protection of Isis.[60]

Worship of Isis was not completely relegated to mystery cults in the Greco-Roman world, however. Every year in March, beginning in the first century CE, the Romans celebrated a public festival called *Navigium Isidis* ("the Ship of Isis").[61] During this festival, which marked the official start to the sailing season, a special boat consecrated to Isis would be launched into the sea in a petition for the goddess's protection of sailors, fishermen, and all those who traveled the waves.[62]

Although the cult of Isis waned as time progressed, it did not disappear entirely. In the eighteenth century, Wolfgang Amadeus Mozart referred to aspects of the Isis mystery cult in his opera *The Magic Flute*, in which the lead character, Tamino, must undergo a series of trials in order to win entry into the Temple of Light, and in which a hymn to Isis and Osiris is sung. More recently, modern pagans have adopted Isis as a deity worthy of reverence. Authors such as Normandi Ellis and de Traci Regula have written books explaining the history of the Isis cult and demonstrating how modern devotees might adapt the worship of Isis to their own spiritual needs.[63]

From her humble beginnings as a native Egyptian funerary goddess and patron of fertility and motherhood, Isis rose to significantly greater stature in the Greco-Roman world than she had held in her own native Egypt. This may be so because it is easy to identify with the goddess's struggles in her myth: her sorrow at the death of her spouse and desire to raise him from the dead, her

---

[60] Antonía Tripolitis, *Religions of the Hellenistic-Roman Age* (Grand Rapids: William B. Eerdmans Publishing Company, 2002), 29.
[61] Laurent Bricault, *Isis Pelagia: Images, Names and Cults of a Goddess of the Seas,* trans. Gil H. Renberg (Leiden: Brill, 2020), 222.
[62] Bricault, *Isis Pelagia,* 228.
[63] de Traci Regula, *The Mysteries of Isis: Her Worship and Magick* (St. Paul: Llewellyn Publications, 2001); Ellis, *Feasts of Light.*

attempts to protect her young son, and her connection with human aspects of life and death through the agricultural cycle and funerary rites. It is no surprise, therefore, that unlike many other ancient deities, Isis has remained a vivid character in the human imagination even five centuries after she first began to be worshiped along the banks of the Nile.

Khnum (Chnum)

Khnum was the god of the source of the Nile, and in some myths was considered to be a creator god. Khnum is usually pictured as a man with the head of a ram. The horns of this ram do not curl in a spiral but rather are wavy and extend out horizontally to the left and right over the ram's head. The primary cult centers for Khnum were at Elephantine, an island in the Nile River just downstream from the First Cataract, and Esna, which is on the west bank of the Nile, south of Luxor.

The identity of Khnum's consort varied depending on location. At Elephantine, Khnum was said to be the husband of Satis, the goddess of war, hunting, and fertility, and the father of Anuket, the goddess of the cataracts of the Nile. At Esna, Khnum's consort was variously Neith or Menhit, who were both war goddesses (although Neith was considerably more popular and powerful), and Khnum's son was Heka, the god of medicine and magic. Khnum was also associated with Hapy, the god of the Nile floods, and was said to be a manifestation of the soul of the sun god, Ra. When Khnum was acting in that capacity, he carried the name Khnum-Ra.

In addition to ensuring the annual flooding of the Nile, Khnum also created the world out of nothing and formed the first human beings on his potter's wheel. He made men and women out of clay and breathed life into them, giving each person a *ba*, or soul. A surviving hymn to Khnum from the temple at Esna details his act of creation, listing various body parts along with their functions, and also stating that Khnum made the plants and the animals.[64]

Although Khnum was worshiped primarily at Elephantine and Esna, he was known and revered throughout Egypt. He is mentioned in the Pyramid Texts, which date from the Fifth Dynasty and which are written on tombs near Saqqara, at the base of the Nile Delta at the opposite end of the river from Khnum's main cult centers. For example, Khnum is said to have built a ferryboat for the pharaoh Unas, and he is credited with having created the pharaoh Teti.[65]

Khnum's importance as a creator and controller of the Nile floods was occasionally harnessed for political purposes. When Queen Hatshepsut assumed the throne following the death of her husband, Pharaoh Thutmose II, she promulgated the myth that Amen was her father and that her body and soul were made by Khnum himself, as part of an effort to legitimize her rule.

Another myth states that when a famine descended upon the land, Pharaoh Djoser had a dream wherein Khnum appeared to him and promised to make the Nile flood so that the famine would stop. In thanks for the god's help, Djoser gave a grant of land and yearly tithes to be paid to Khnum's temple. It is unclear whether the story about Djoser actually dates from the Third Dynasty, since it is preserved on a stele that dates from Ptolemaic times. It is possible that the story is actually from Ptolemaic Egypt but was forged to make it seem older, in order to give it more weight and importance.

---

[64] Lichtheim, *Literature* 3, 112–13.
[65] Allen, *Pyramid Texts*, pp. 55, 68.

Khonsu (Khons, Chons)

Khonsu, whose name means "traveler," was the Egyptian god of the moon. He is usually depicted as a mummy with a child's shaved head and braided sidelock, although sometimes he is shown as a man with a falcon's head wearing a headdress in which the moon disk is set. One of Khonsu's main cult centers was the city of Thebes. In Thebes, as well as in the rest of southern Egypt, Khonsu was part of the Theban Triad, in which the god Amen was Khonsu's father and the goddess Mut was his mother. Within the great temple of Amen in Karnak, Khonsu has his own precinct. In the northern part of Egypt, however, Khonsu was in a triad with his parents Ptah and Sekhmet, while in the Fayum, his parents were said to be Hathor and Sobek.

As a moon good, Khonsu was sometimes associated with Thoth, and therefore was seen as a god of calendars and timekeeping. In the myth of the birth of the children of Nut, Khonsu loses at dice to Thoth, and as a result, he has to forfeit a fifth of his light. Thoth uses that light to make the five intercalary days that were added to the 360-day lunar calendar in order to keep it aligned with the seasons.

Egyptologist Geraldine Price notes that the earliest mentions of Khonsu paint him as a god to be feared, because he "strangled lesser deities and ate the hearts of the dead."[66] He was also feared because of his role as Keeper of the Books of the End of the Year, a list of all the people who were destined to die during that year.[67] When Khonsu played that role, he was thought to take on the shape of a baboon, another aspect that he shares with Thoth.

Sometimes Khonsu's ferocity was called upon to cast out demons and heal the sick. We see this in one of the primary myths about Khonsu, which is preserved in a fourth-century BCE inscription that details how he healed a princess from demonic possession. In the story, a princess from a country called Bekhten becomes very ill because a demon has taken hold of her. Pharaoh Rameses II, who is married to the princess's sister, is asked for help, so he sends his learned men to Bekhten to see what might be done. The most learned and skilled of all these wise men tries his best to cure the young woman, but soon discovers that he has no power over the demon. The learned men return home, sorrowful that they could not help.

When Rameses hears what happened, he goes to the Temple of Khonsu to ask for aid. The priests of the temple suggest taking a statue of the god to Bekhten so that the god can fight the demon. Khonsu agrees to go, so Rameses sends him to Bekhten with a great retinue, and the god is immediately brought before the afflicted princess. Khonsu has a conversation with the demon, who demands that the people of Bekhten hold a festival in his honor if they want him to leave. Khonsu decides that this is a reasonable request and agrees to the demon's terms. The king of Bekhten also agrees, and so the demon leaves, after which the king holds the feast as he promised. Once the festival is completed, the princess is well again, upon which the king orders another festival, this time to celebrate the princess's return to health and to give thanks to Khonsu for his help.

---

[66] Pinch, *Handbook*, 155.
[67] Pinch, *Handbook*, 155.

After the festival of thanksgiving, the Egyptian priests ask leave to depart, but the king doesn't want them to go because he's afraid the demon might come back once Khonsu leaves. The priests then make a shrine for Khonsu in Bekhten, where he is greatly honored. The priests and Khonsu spend three years in Bekhten, at the end of which the god appears to the king in a dream and tells him that he wants to go home. The king is saddened by this, but he understands what he must do. He gives the priests many gifts for themselves and other treasures besides for them to put in Khonsu's temple in Egypt. The priests take the god home, and everyone lives in peace thereafter.

Maat (Ma'at, Ma'et, Mayet)

The goddess Maat was the personification of justice, law, cosmic order, and right living, and as such was one of the most important deities in the Egyptian pantheon. She is often portrayed as a beautiful woman wearing a dress and a headband in which an ostrich feather has been placed. Maat was not only a goddess, however; as a moral, religious, and legal concept, *maat* played a vital role in Egyptian kingship and in the daily life of all Egyptians. Egyptologist Geraldine Pinch notes that "[t]he primary duty of an Egyptian king was to be the champion of *maat*. In the afterlife, the dead were judged on whether they had done and spoken *maat*."[68] This judgment was accomplished by weighing the heart of the deceased person against the goddess Maat's ostrich feather. A just heart would be equal in weight to the feather, or even lighter, while an evil heart would be heavier. The person with a just heart would be allowed to go on to paradise, while those who had evil hearts were consumed by Ammit.

Maat was usually seen as the wife of Thoth and the daughter of Ra, and was said to travel with Ra in his solar barge. Author Veronica Ions notes that Maat, when part of the crew of Ra's barque,

---

[68] Pinch, *Handbook*, 159.

represented "[t]he light which Ra brought into the world ... he created the world by putting her in the place of chaos."[69]

But Maat was more than Ra's creature: she was also the basis for Ra's own power. Visual representations of this sometimes show Ra sitting on a small plinth, which represents Maat. Maat is the foundation upon which Ra sits, and therefore, she represents the foundation of cosmic order. The depiction of Maat as a plinth that supports a god is not limited to Ra. Osiris and Ptah are also frequently shown standing on this platform, which visually reinforced their own authority and dedication to justice and order.

---

[69] Veronica Ions, *Egyptian Mythology* (New York: Peter Bedrick Books, 1990), 113.

Nefertem (Nefertum)

The word "nefer" means "beautiful" in ancient Egyptian, and the god Nefertem was associated particularly with the beauty of the lotus flower. Because of the lotus's sweet scent, Nefertem was also the god of perfumes. In the Memphite Triad, Nefertem was the son of Ptah and Sekhmet. Nefertem is often depicted as a beautiful young man, sometimes with the head of a lion, with a lotus flower headdress. Because of this association with the lotus, Nefertem was also connected in the Egyptian religious imagination to aspects of the creation of the universe and to the creator god Ra.

One ancient Egyptian creation story says that, in the beginning, there was only a lotus floating on the waters of Nun. When the lotus opened, the sun god Ra was born from inside it. Egyptologist Geraldine Pinch states that the connection between the sun and the lotus flower in this creation myth likely comes from observations of the lotus's behavior. It only opens during the day, and it is pollinated by beetles, an insect that was considered to be a form of Khepera, the god of the rising sun.[70]

---

[70] Pinch, *Handbook*, 158.

Neith (Neit)

The goddess Neith had her primary cult center in the city of Sais in the Nile Delta. Her name seems to mean "the terrifying one," and her primary symbol appears to represent two arrows crossed over a shield. These attributes suggest that she originally was a warlike deity. Neith is sometimes depicted as a woman wearing a dress, with the cartouche-shaped symbol just mentioned on her head, while at other times she is shown wearing the red crown of Lower Egypt. She was a goddess of weaving, mothers, and wisdom, and she was also considered to be a creator deity.

In her role as a creator, Neith had nonbinary gender. Geraldine Pinch states that Neith was referred to as "Mother and Father of All Things," a deity who "created the world by speaking seven magical words."[71] This version of the creation myth is preserved at the Temple of Khnum at Esna. In this myth, Neith emerges from the primeval waters, creates the primeval mound, and then speaks creation into being.[72]

Neith was the mother of the crocodile god Sobek and was considered to be one of the great mother goddesses of Egypt. She

---

[71] Pinch, *Handbook*, 170.
[72] Barbara Watterson, *The Gods of Ancient Egypt* (New York: Facts on File, Inc., 1984), 176.

was respected for her wisdom, and in the myth "The Battle of Horus and Set," the gods appeal to her to settle the dispute over who should be the king of Egypt. Her reply in support of Horus is curt and no-nonsense, as is the wont of older women who are fed up with the squabbling of children.

Nephthys (Nebt-het)

Nephthys was the daughter of the earth god Geb and the sky goddess Nut. Even though she was the sister to Isis, Osiris, and Set, Nephthys often takes on a secondary role in most myths. However, her role is still very important; it is with Nephthys's help that Isis is able to reassemble the pieces of her dismembered husband and bring him back to life. For this reason, Nephthys was associated with death and funerals, and she is often depicted standing alongside the bier with Isis. Further, as a goddess of weaving, Nephthys was specifically associated with the weaving of linen wrappings for mummies.

Nephthys was nominally married to her brother Set, just as Isis was paired off with Osiris. Nephthys's marriage does not seem to have been a happy one; at one point she seduces Osiris, and Anubis is born from that union. Nephthys is more commonly depicted as spending time with Isis rather than Set in both myths and various ancient illustrations of mythical scenes.

Together with Isis, Nephthys had the function of a mourner at a funeral. This is shown in the funerary texts mentioned above, but especially in a surviving text known as "The Lamentations of Isis and Nephthys," in which the two goddesses mourn for the slain Osiris. This text came to be performed during rites commemorating the death of Osiris, and it eventually came to be included as part of the *Book of the Dead.*

Nun (Noun, Nu)

To the ancient Egyptians, Nun was simultaneously a place, a substance, a concept, and a deity. Nun was the primordial waters from which all creation arose, both as the substance of the waters themselves and as the place where those waters resided. Nun was the place in which the universe began and a place that continued to exist even after the world was made. The creator god Atum came into being in the middle of Nun, and it is in Nun that he gave birth to his children Shu and Tefnut, the air and the light of the world. As a concept, Nun represented insubstantiality and formlessness, while as a deity, Nun was the frog-headed personification of both the primordial waters and of formlessness, existing alongside his snake-headed consort Naunet as part of the Hermopolitan Ogdoad, the collection of eight deities who arose from nothingness to undertake the first acts of creation.

Nun was not just a god of the past, nor did Nun cease to be of cosmological importance once the world was created. Even after the universe had been brought fully to life, Nun played important roles in the Egyptian understanding of how the world worked. Nun flowed through the Underworld, and Nun was the origin of the waters of the Nile. Various deities and demons dwelt in Nun, from where they could arise to help or hinder humans. For example, the great serpent

Apep (Apophis) dwelt in Nun and had to be vanquished every night lest he devour the sun as it made its transit from west to east on the waters of the Underworld, and when the boat of Ra made that transit safely, some myths claimed that it was the waters of Nun that raised up the sun in the morning.

In addition to the omnipresent Nile, other waters were used as physical representations of Nun in ancient Egyptian religious architecture and practice. For example, because the vulture goddess Nekhebet also inhabited Nun, her temple at Elkab had a sacred lake representing the primordial waters.

Waters representing Nun were an important part of the pharaoh's daily routine. Every morning when the pharaoh arose, a ceremony called the "Rite of the House of Morning" was performed, in which the pharaoh was bathed and dressed for the day. The water used for the bathing was taken from a sacred source and represented Nun. Being bathed in the waters of Nun was thought to represent the rebirth of the pharaoh, an echo of Ra's journey across Nun in the Underworld to be reborn every morning as the rising sun. In this way, the pharaoh's body was aligned with that of Ra and made to participate in the god's own activities.

The Ogdoad of Hermopolis

The Ogdoad was a set of eight primeval gods worshiped at Khemenu in central Egypt. Khemenu literally means "Eight Town," a reference to the Ogdoad, but today we are more familiar with its Greek name: Hermopolis ("City of Hermes"). The Ogdoad was made up of four pairs of deities, with each pair consisting of a god and his consort. The gods were usually depicted as men with frogs' heads, while the goddesses were shown as women with serpents' heads. Each divine pair represented a different cosmic concept, as described in the table below:

Deities	Concept
Amen and Amaunet	Hiddenness
Heh and Hauhet	Eternity
Kek and Kekhet	Darkness
Nun and Naunet	Primeval waters

According to the Hermopolitan creation story, these eight deities created the world out of a primeval mound that stood in the waters of Nun. These primordial waters were represented by a sacred lake at the main temple in Hermopolis, and a small island in the middle of the lake was said to be the primeval mound itself. The myth goes on to state that once the Ogdoad had created the world, they ruled over it for a time, then died and went into the Underworld, where they continued to cause the Nile to flow and the sun to rise.

Although the Ogdoad were important creator deities in Hermopolis, the Hermopolitan creation myth in fact had four other variants:

> A celestial goose called the "Great Cackler" lays an egg on the primeval mound; the egg contains the god Ra, who then goes on to create the world.

> Similar to the first version, but the bird laying the cosmic egg is an ibis, representing the god Thoth (identified with Hermes by the Greeks, which is the origin of the name "Hermopolis").

> A lotus flower rises out of the primeval waters, and when it opens, Ra is born from inside it.

> Similar to the third version, but it is a scarab beetle inside the lotus, and when the beetle weeps, humans are created.

Of the deities in the Ogdoad, Amen and Nun both went on to have important places in the mythology and religion of Egypt as a whole, while the others were worshiped primarily at Hermopolis.

Osiris

Osiris, the dying and rising god, was one of the most important deities in the Egyptian pantheon. The eldest child of the sky goddess Nut and the earth god Geb, Osiris was credited with bringing civilization to human beings, teaching them agriculture and law, and giving them grain to grow and eat. Osiris was both the brother and the husband of the goddess Isis, who assisted him in his work during his life. Following his dismemberment by his jealous brother Set and his later resurrection by Isis, Osiris descended into the Tuat, or Underworld, where he became the god of the dead and the judge of souls.

Osiris's name in Egyptian is *Usir*, which means "powerful." ("Osiris" is a Latin version of the name.) Osiris was closely associated with the agricultural cycle, and especially with the risings and fallings of the Nile, upon which all Egyptian agriculture depended. In his guise as the god of the dead, Osiris is often depicted as having green skin and swathed in a mummy's bands, wearing the white, feathered *atef* crown and holding the scepter and flail that were the symbols of Egyptian kingship. The greenness of his skin is not connected to death, but rather is a reference to his lifegiving power through his control of the inundations of the Nile. Other representations of Osiris show him as a normal human being, dressed as an Egyptian pharaoh.

The primary Osiris myth states that when Osiris ruled over Egypt long, long ago, his brother Seth became jealous of his power and arranged to kill him by sealing him inside a specially made coffin and tossing it into the Nile. The coffin washes up on the shores of the city of Byblos, where it becomes lodged in the roots of a growing tamarisk tree. When the tamarisk is fully grown, the king of Byblos cuts it down to use as a pillar in his palace, completely unaware of the god concealed inside. Osiris's sister-wife, Isis, goes on a journey looking for her husband. She manages to locate the tamarisk tree and free Osiris's body from it. With the help of other gods, she resurrects Osiris, but this second life doesn't last long. Seth finds Osiris and kills him again, this time chopping his body up into fourteen pieces that he scatters throughout the land. Isis goes looking for the pieces of her husband's body, and she finds all but the penis, which had been thrown into the Nile and devoured by a fish. Isis puts Osiris back together by mummifying his body, but this time he cannot stay in the land of the living; he instead goes down into the Tuat, where he reigns as king.

The origins of the Osiris cult are both ancient and complex. It is often assumed that he has his origins in the ancient city of Djedu in the Nile Delta, where he may have been conflated with a local fertility god named Andjeti.[73] Originally, Osiris was a relatively minor god, considered secondary to the sun god, Ra, but as time wore on, Osiris gradually eclipsed Ra in some respects and became one of the primary deities of the Egyptian pantheon. This change did not take place overnight; although it is possible Osiris was worshiped in the earlier dynasties of the Old Kingdom, it is not until the Fifth Dynasty Pyramid Texts that we see him being treated as the lord of the dead and facilitator of the resurrection of the king. It is also during the Fifth Dynasty that we see Osiris's new importance within Egyptian religion.

---

[73] Ions, Egyptian Mythology, 126.

Egyptologist Rosalie David notes that as the Osiris cult grew in popularity, there was a shift in the Egyptian understanding of the afterlife. According to David, paradise was initially accessible only by the pharaohs, but during the Middle Kingdom, this exclusive club was opened to other Egyptian nobles.[74] The democratization of the afterlife continued until eventually people from all walks of life were thought to be able to enter into paradise if they had lived good lives.

The Osiris cult, once established, was centered primarily in the southern city of Abydos, near the modern-day town of El Bayana, with a less important shrine in the city of Busiris (now Abu Sir Bana) in the central Nile Delta. Abydos was traditionally thought to be the place where Osiris's head landed after his dismemberment by Set, and Busiris the place to which Set flung Osiris's spine. Located along the Nile in Upper Egypt, Abydos had a number of temple complexes and also a royal necropolis, which was used for the burials of early pharaohs. Burial in a place sacred to Osiris likely reflected the wish that the person being buried would be resurrected just as the god had been.

According to Egyptologist E. A. Wallace Budge, the temple at Abydos was constructed during the Twelfth Dynasty at the command of Pharaoh Senusret III.[75] Budge notes that a description of this temple survives in the text of a stele made by Ikhernefert, the official commissioned with its construction. In addition to the temple building, which the stele reports was made "from sweet-smelling woods, and inlaid with gold, silver, and lapis-lazuli," Ikhernefert caused a new statue of the god and a new neshmet boat to be made. The neshmet boat was both the sacred boat in which Osiris sailed in his journey through the Underworld, as described in the *Book of the*

[74] A. Rosalie David, *The Ancient Egyptians: Religious Beliefs and Practices* (London: Routledge & Kegan Paul, 1982), 73.
[75] E. A. Wallace Budge, *Osiris and the Egyptian Resurrection*, vol. 2 (London: P. L. Warner, [1911]), 4.

Dead, and also a physical object in the world of the living, which was a part of sacred processions in honor of the god.[76]

A basic outline of some of the rites of Osiris also survives on the stele of Ikhernefert. Ikhernefert says that the statue of the god was richly dressed and placed inside its neshmet boat, which then was taken on a long procession that involved several stages that occurred as follows:[77]

> 1. A procession involving the jackal-headed funerary god Wepwawet (not to be confused with Anubis), who functioned during this festival as a stand-in for or avatar of Osiris's son, Horus
>
> 2. A mock attack on Osiris's neshmet boat as it leaves its sanctuary in Abydos, in which the attackers are repelled
>
> 3. The procession of the neshmet boat moves eastward from Abydos to Peqer (now Umm Al Qa'ab), the location of the royal necropolis, representing Osiris's death
>
> 4. Another mock battle on the riverbank, in which Osiris's followers are victorious (although the ancient historian Herodotus claims that sometimes these mock battles descended into actual violence)[78]
>
> 5. A procession to return the neshmet boat to Abydos
>
> 6. Various purification rites inside the temple of the god to close out the festival

---

[76] Budge, *Egyptian Resurrection*, 2, 4; see also Martyn Smith, *Religion, Culture, and Sacred Space* (New York: Palgrave MacMillan, 2008), 53–4.

[77] Smith, Religion, Culture, and Sacred Space, 54–55.

[78] Herodotus II:63; Cary, trans., 119.

The stele of Ikhernefert also preserves some intriguing hints about Ikhernefert's other activities with respect to establishing Osiris's new temple. Apparently Ikhernefert had been charged with reforming the worship of Osiris in addition to his construction work, since he claims to have instructed "the hour priests of the temple so that they might do their duties and know the rituals that pertain to each day and the festivals at the start of the seasons."[79]

In addition to presiding over the Tuat and judging the souls of the dead, Osiris was inextricably linked with fertility. In ancient Egypt, this meant being linked with the yearly flood cycle of the Nile, which continued into the twentieth century CE until the construction of dams and a system of canals along the river put a stop to the inundations. Prior to modern times, the Nile's yearly flood cycle began around the middle of August when monsoons that began the previous May in the Ethiopian highlands dumped an enormous quantity of water into the Nile and other rivers in the area. The swollen river would rise through the end of August and reach its peak in September, after which it would begin to recede, leaving a layer of enormously fertile sediment behind. The receding of the flood reached its lowest point in April, and in the following August, the cycle would begin again.

For the ancient Egyptians, the annual floods were integral not only to the agricultural calendar but also to the religious one, which connected the flood itself and the fecundity it promoted to the person of and myths about Osiris. In his role as a god of fertility, Osiris was linked with the life cycle of grain crops, the success of which was bound up with the cycle of floods. Ancient Egyptians believed that just as Osiris died and came back to life twice, so too did the seed "die" when it was sown only to rise back up and be cut down again at harvest time, when it would "die" again through being transformed into food products such as bread and beer.[80] Worshipers would even

---

[79] Translation in Smith, Religion, Culture, and Sacred Space, 53.
[80] Henri Frankfort, *Ancient Egyptian Religion: An Interpretation* (New York:

make little effigies of the mummified Osiris, stuffed with seeds, which they would then plant and tend. However, not only was the grain that grew from the Nile's muddy bounty aligned with Osiris, but as Veronica Ions states, the floodwaters themselves were also considered to be the "sweat of Osiris's hands and the tears that Isis shed into the river."[81]

The myth of Osiris's death and subsequent resurrection has led some scholars to attempt to show a direct line of descent between ancient Egyptian religion and Christianity, the latter of which centers around the death and resurrection of Jesus of Nazareth. However, scholarly opinion is divided as to whether this lineage exists. The death and resurrection stories certainly would seem to run in parallel, at least up to a point. A second parallel might be that Osiris was considered to be somehow embodied in the grain consumed by his followers, while according to some Christian sects, Jesus's essence is said to be contained in the eucharistic bread because of the words of institution—"this is my body"—uttered at the Last Supper.[82] And Jesus is seen as a guide and savior who can restore the souls of the dead to an everlasting life that is open to all people, regardless of station, a role he shares with Osiris.

Whether there is an actual organic connection between the Osiris cult and the establishment of Christianity remains an open question, but the adaptation and transformation of the Osiris cult within the context of Egyptian religion during the Ptolemaic Period in Egypt is not. Osiris was combined with the Apis bull by Ptolemy I into a new deity known as Serapis, and the worship of Osiris as a god in his own right gradually faded out, although rites were still being performed at the temple complex in Philae until the middle of the fifth century CE, when pagan practices were outlawed in favor of Christianity.

Harper & Row, 1948), 28.
[81] Ions, Egyptian Mythology, 108.
[82] Mark 14:22–25; Luke 22:18–20.

As was the case in Hellenized Egypt, Osiris has received less attention than Isis and Thoth from modern occultists and pagans, although scholarly interest in Osiris as a god of death and resurrection became renewed during the late nineteenth century, when Sir James George Frazer published *The Golden Bough*, a comparative study of world religions.[83] In that study, Frazer connected Osiris with other gods such as Tammuz/Dumuzi, an ancient Mesopotamian god, and Attis, a Phrygian deity. However, scholars have since disputed many of Frazer's claims, stating that they are not supported by the evidence.[84]

---

[83] James George Frazer, *The Golden Bough: A Study in Magic and Religion*, third ed. Part IV, Vol. 11, *Adonis Attis Osiris* (London: The MacMillan Press, Ltd., 1914).

[84] See, for example, Paul Rhodes Eddy and Gregory A. Boyd, *The Jesus Legend: A Case for the Historical Reliability of the Synoptic Jesus Tradition* (Grand Rapids: Baker Academic, 2007), 143.

Ptah

The supreme god of the city of Memphis was Ptah. In the Memphite cosmogony, Ptah is the creator god from whom all other gods spring at the beginning of creation. First, Ptah (who is also identified with Nun, the primeval waters) creates Atum, and then Atum goes on to create the Ennead, a collection of nine gods worshiped primarily at Heliopolis. Ptah also creates the world and sets the land of Egypt in order. Some scholars think that the elevation of Ptah to supreme creator might have been an attempt on the part of his priests in Memphis to create a hierarchy in which the chief gods of Heliopolis were made subordinate to Memphis's own.[85]

Ptah is usually depicted as a man wearing a tight skullcap and straight beard. He holds the *was* scepter, which was the symbol of power and authority in Egypt. This scepter has two small horns at its foot and a hook with a kind of antler at the top. Some images of Ptah show his body swathed tightly in the linen wrappings of a mummy, with green skin on his face and hands. Ptah's consort is the lion-headed goddess Sekhmet, and their son is Nefertem, who was said to have originated as a lotus flower and who was associated with fragrance and perfumes.

---

[85] Hart, *Dictionary*, 129.

Ptah was the patron of craftsmen in ancient Egypt. Egyptologist George Hart reports that images of craftsmen praying to Ptah survive on stelae at what is now Deir el-Medina. These stelae were made by the workers who did sculpting work for tombs in the Valley of the Kings.[86] This connection between Ptah and craftsmanship perhaps reached its peak in the person of Imhotep, who served during the Third Dynasty as the master sculptor to Pharaoh Djoser, and who may have been the architect of Djoser's step pyramid. Imhotep's reputation for wisdom and integrity eventually led him to be deified, at which point he was often referred to as the "son of Ptah." (See the chapter on Imhotep above.)

---

[86] Hart, *Dictionary*, 130-31.

Ra (Re, Pre)

Ra was the Egyptian god of the sun, an all-powerful creator who rode in the Barque of Millions of Years across the sky each day to bring light and life to the earth. At night, the barque descended into the Underworld, where Ra and his crew had to brave various dangers in order to get to the other side so that the sun might rise again in the morning. The chief enemy of Ra was the great serpent Apep (Apophis), who had to be slain each night. Ra's chief cult center was in the city of Heliopolis, and he eventually became identified with the creator god Atum. Egyptologist Leonard Lesko observes that Ra's cult was so influential and powerful that it eventually appropriated both the Heliopolitan and Hermopolitan cosmologies, integrating them into the mythology about Ra's origins, powers, and role within the pantheon.[87]

One example of this association with the Heliopolitan cosmology comes from the *Book of the Dead*. In that text, Atum, the primary god of the Heliopolitan Ennead, is the manifestation of the creator at the beginning of creation, just following his emergence from the primordial waters, while Ra is his manifestation in the person of the

---

[87] Leonard H. Lesko, "Ancient Egyptian Cosmogonies and Cosmology," in *Religion in Ancient Egypt: Gods, Myths, and Personal Practice*, ed. by Byron E. Shafer (Ithaca: Cornell University Press, 1991), 115.

---

sun god and as the sun itself.[88] In creation myths, therefore, Atum and Ra become interchangeable versions of the same deity.

Ra also had multiple forms in his manifestation as the sun. Ra-Horakhty represented the sun at midday, while Ra-Atum was the setting sun and Khepera the rising sun in the morning. Each of these forms had their own visual representations. Khepera was the scarab beetle, who pushed the sun above the horizon in much the same way that these beetles push balls of dung around. Ra-Horakhty was pictured as a man with a falcon's head, and Ra-Atum was pictured as a human man wearing the double crown of Egypt. In addition, Ra was sometimes said to become Osiris at night, when he traveled through the Underworld.

Although each of these representations show a male figure, the manifestation of Ra's power, the Eye of Ra, was conceived of as female. The Eye was both part of Ra and separate from him. He could detach it and send it to do his bidding, and when he did so, it was in the form of a goddess, such as Hathor or Sekhmet. We see this in the myth in which Ra decides to destroy all of humanity because they are leading evil lives and not worshiping the gods properly. To achieve this, Ra sends his Eye in the form of Hathor (who is also Sekhmet) to kill all the people and to ravage their lands. Because the Eye was separate from Ra, he did not always exercise full control over it. In the "Distant Goddess" myth, Ra's Eye (again in the form of a goddess such as Hathor) runs away into the desert and has to be fetched back and reunited with Ra.

The living embodiment of the *ba*, or spirit, of Ra was the Mnevis bull, a sacred bull that was kept at the temple of Ra in Heliopolis. This animal was usually all black, and had two cows to serve as his wives. The cows were said to represent the goddesses Hathor, who often functioned as the Eye of Ra, and Iusas, a goddess said to be the hand of Atum that worked to produce the seed from which all creation was made. When the Mnevis bull died, it was mummified

---

[88] Lesko, "Cosmogonies and Cosmology," 113.

and buried with great ceremony. Egyptologist Barbara Watterson notes that the Mnevis bull remained a popular and important aspect of the worship of Ra well into the Ptolemaic Period.[89]

In some myths, Ra is portrayed as weak and old, or else as vacillating, peevish, and unwilling to say aloud what he really believes. In the story about how Isis learned Ra's true name, Ra is described as an incontinent old man who has lost all of his teeth, and Isis tortures him with venomous snake bites until he relents and tells her his name. In "The Battle of Horus and Set," Ra-Horakhty is the king of the gods, but when the matter at hand isn't settled either quickly or to his liking, he goes off into his tent to sulk. Further, Ra-Horakhty supports Set's claim to the throne, but will not come forth to order that Set be given the crown; in fact, he is described as secretly supporting Set over Horus. In this tale, Ra-Horakhty lacks the courage of his convictions, and he proposes several maneuvers intended to get others to make the decision for him.

Ra was often syncretized with other deities. Amen-Ra was one especially important syncretization in the New Kingdom. Other syncretizations included Sobek-Ra and Khnum-Ra.

---

[89] Watterson, Gods of Ancient Egypt, 68.

Serapis (Sarapis, Userhapi)

Unlike the other gods in the Egyptian pantheon, Serapis was not a product of the native Egyptian religious imagination. Serapis did not grow out of the native Egyptian understanding of the world or its origins, nor was he allied to native Egyptian ideas about social and political structures. Instead, Serapis was a deity purpose-built by Ptolemy I, the Greek successor to Alexander the Great, who wished to find some way to fuse Greek and Egyptian religious expression and so lend legitimacy to the rule of Egypt by her Greek conquerors.

Serapis was in part a syncretization of the god Osiris and the Apis bull. The Apis bull was worshiped particularly in Memphis, where he was said to be the son of Hathor and the herald of Ptah, and where he was a symbol of the ruling pharaoh. Worship of the Apis bull had been a feature of Egyptian religion at least since the First Dynasty, and the worship of Osiris became commonplace during the Fifth, so both were already well entrenched in the Egyptian pantheon by the time the Ptolemies came to power.

In addition to this syncretization of ancient Egyptian deities, Ptolemy tacked Greek characteristics onto Serapis to round out the new god's appeal to both Greeks and Egyptians. For example, when images of Serapis were made, they were constructed along the same lines as other contemporary Greek representations of religious and political figures. Serapis therefore is depicted realistically as a muscular adult male with long curly hair and a beard, often with a basket on top of his head, and he shared certain features with Greek gods such as Zeus, Dionysus, and Hades.

This association with Hades, who in Rome was known as Pluto, is attested to in the writings of the ancient historian Plutarch, who also states that Serapis was brought to Egypt by Ptolemy I as the result of a dream.[90] In the dream, the statue of Pluto at Sinope tells Ptolemy to take him from Sinope and bring him to Alexandria. The statue supposedly included a representation of Pluto's three-headed dog Cerberus. Plutarch goes on to say that when the statue arrived in Alexandria, Ptolemy declared it to be a representation of Serapis.

In order to form the traditional Egyptian triad, Serapis was said to be the husband of Isis and the father of Horus. The form of Horus used was that of Harpocrates, the winged child deity who was the god of secrets and who had already found favor among Greek worshipers. Although the Egyptian priests in Heliopolis attempted to integrate Serapis into their religious thought by positing that Serapis was created when the soul of the Apis bull entered the afterlife and merged with Osiris, Serapis never really found much favor among the native Egyptian populace, who preferred to worship their own traditional gods.[91]

Serapis was much more popular outside of Egypt, especially in Rome. In Rome, Serapis was worshiped alongside Isis, who had a temple that had been built by Emperor Caligula in the Campus Martius, an important area in ancient Rome that housed public baths and the temple known as the Pantheon, which is still intact and may be visited today.

The Roman emperor Vespasian particularly seems to have made use of the power attributed to Serapis in order to boost his own

---

[90] C. W. King, trans. *Plutarch's Morals: Theosophical Essays* (London: George Bell & Sons, 1889), 22–23.
[91] Ions, Egyptian Mythology, 122.

popularity and authority, particularly within Egypt, which at that time was part of the Roman Empire. The ancient historian Tacitus reports that while Vespasian was visiting Alexandria, a blind man and a man with a disabled hand came to Vespasian saying that Serapis had sent them to the emperor to be healed.[92] At first Vespasian scoffed at this, but then he did what the two disabled men asked, and they were healed. According to Tacitus, Vespasian then made it a point to go to the Serapeum, or temple to Serapis, where he ordered everyone else to leave so that he might consult the god alone. There Vespasian had a vision, which he considered to have been sent by Serapis himself.

Serapis was of sufficient importance in imperial Rome that he often was depicted on coins. Coinage from the reigns of Vespasian and some later emperors feature the face of the emperor in profile on one side and an image of Serapis, sometimes accompanied by Isis, on the other.

---

[92] Cornelius Tacitus, The Works of Tacitus: The Oxford Translation, Revised, vol. 2: The History, Germany, Agricola, and Dialogue on Orations (New York: Harper & Brothers, Publishers, 1858),

Set (Seth, Sutekh)

Set is one of the oldest Egyptian gods, having been worshiped in the Predynastic Period. Set also is an ambivalent character, representing both good and evil. Whether his role is good or bad depends partly on the time period and partly on the activity in which Set is engaged at the time. He was the murderer of his brother Osiris and a pretender to the throne of Egypt, but he also rode in the prow of the solar barge and killed Apep, the giant serpent that threatened to devour the sun every night.

The god of chaos, thunder, and deserts, Set is depicted as a man with the head of a strange animal that has never been definitively identified. The Set-animal is black in color, with a long, narrow snout and two upright, rectangular ears. Some scholars have said that the Set-animal is a composite creature made up of parts from other animals, while others have suggested that it might represent a type of dog resembling the modern Saluki.

In Egyptian myth, Set is depicted as jealous and ruthless, willing to murder, maim, and rape in order to get his way. By the New Kingdom, Set is also depicted as being more brawn than brain; we see this especially in the story "The Battle of Horus and Set," where he is easily fooled by Horus and Isis, who are just as willing to cheat as Set is.

Perhaps the most famous story in which Set appears is that of Isis and Osiris. In this story, which is variously summarized in the above chapters on the latter two deities, Set contrives to murder Osiris not once but twice in order to steal his throne. In the second instance, Set dismembers Osiris, and because Osiris's penis is consumed by a fish, Osiris will never be whole again, despite the heroic efforts of Isis, Anubis, Thoth, and other deities who work together to resurrect him.

In the story in which Set contends with Horus for the throne, summarized in the chapter on Horus above, Set is unwilling to accept the judgment of the court of the gods, and proposes various contests between himself and Horus to see who ought to have the throne of Egypt. Neither contest is ever decided in favor of one or the other, because Horus and his mother Isis try to cheat and thus skew the results. Set, on the other hand, for all that he may be murderous and rather stupid, tries to follow the rules when he accepts these challenges.

Rules go out the window, however, when Set sees an opportunity to discredit Horus first by attempting to rape him and then by trying to shame him by saying publicly that the sex was consensual. This trick backfires when Set ends up ejaculating into Horus's hands. Horus then enlists the help of his mother to show that Set was lying about what actually happened. Set likewise takes advantage of an opportunity to maim Horus while the latter is sleeping and therefore defenseless, but Horus is eventually restored to health by Hathor.

Early in Egyptian history, Set was worshiped primarily in Upper Egypt, where he had a cult center at Kom Ombo. Set later was worshiped throughout the country, and several pharaohs had a particular devotion to him. Eventually, however, Set began to be seen more as a force for evil and fell out of favor. Egyptologist Geraldine Pinch reports that starting in the New Kingdom, Egyptian religion began to concentrate more on Set's crimes, such that the priests of Horus at Edfu "celebrated a day of castrating Seth and 'reducing him to pieces' in retaliation for Seth's mutilation of the body of Osiris and the Eye of Horus."[93] The process of demonizing Set continued from the New Kingdom onward and, as Pinch states, reached its peak during the Greco-Roman period, at which point, "Seth was vilified in most temples."[94]

---

[93] Pinch, *Handbook*, 193.
[94] Pinch, *Handbook*, 193.

Sobek (Suchos)

The crocodile-headed Sobek was a god of the waters and of fertility and the son of the mother goddess Neith. Sobek originally was a deity specific to the Fayum region, which in ancient times was a marshy oasis, located about sixty miles south of what is now Cairo. During the Twelfth Dynasty, pharaohs such as Amenemhat III worked to harness the water of the Fayum region by creating a canal from the Nile into Lake Moeris, which seems to have been used as a kind of reservoir that could be drawn on in times of drought. The chief settlement in the Fayum in ancient times was Shedet, known in Greek as Crocodilopolis.

Crocodiles are native to the Nile, and since ancient Egyptians often associated particular animals with particular deities, it should be no surprise that a crocodile god should have been worshiped in a region known for its wetlands. Ancient temples to Sobek even kept living crocodiles as exemplars of the god. The priests cared for the animals carefully and embalmed them for proper burial when they died. Examinations of mummified adult crocodiles have even found sets of mummified babies in the mouths of the adults, likely a representation of one way in which living crocodiles care for their young. Egyptologist Salima Ikram speculates that "the insertion of babies in this manner was intented [*sic*] to emphasize the positive nurturing and caring aspect of this fearsome beast."[95]

In addition to his cult in the Fayum, Sobek had a major temple at Kom Ombo, which lies about halfway between Edfu and Aswan. At Kom Ombo, Sobek was revered along with Horus. Horus was given one side of the temple, while Sobek had the other, and each god was given an avatar of Hathor as his consort. Horus's son was the god Pantebtawy, "Lord of the Two Lands," while Sobek was given the moon god Khonsu to be his child.[96] However, Egyptologist Barbara Watterson notes that this combination comes with a certain amount of dissonance, as Horus's traditional enemy, the evil god Set, often took the form of a crocodile.[97] Watterson posits that the cult of Sobek at Kom Ombo was intended to be a stand-in for the worship of Set, whose cult had been outlawed.[98]

---

[95] Salima Ikram, "Protecting Pets and Cleaning Crocodiles: The Animal Mummy Project," in *Divine Creatures: Animal Mummies in Ancient Egypt*, edited by Salima Ikram (Cairo: The American University of Cairo Press, 2005), 219.
[96] Watterson, Gods of Ancient Egypt, 121.
[97] Watterson, Gods of Ancient Egypt, 121.
[98] Watterson, Gods of Ancient Egypt, 122.

Thoth

In Egyptian mythology, Thoth held a position of great importance as the creator of writing and law, and as the god who oversaw the calendar and ordered the times and the seasons. Today, many people are familiar with the depiction of Thoth as a man with the head of an ibis, but in ancient Egypt he was also depicted in the form of a baboon, sometimes with a lunar disk over its head and sometimes without. As with other Egyptian deities, Thoth was adopted by devotees from outside of Egypt, eventually becoming syncretized with the Greek messenger god Hermes. Thoth's association with magic and knowledge also attracted the interest of alchemists, magicians, and occultists in both the Renaissance and in more modern times.

There is no single myth describing Thoth's origins. Depending on the source, he is variously said to have emerged into being through his own power or to have been spoken into being by the sun god Ra. In the former myth, Thoth is also the creator of the universe, an act that he accomplishes in his ibis-form by laying the egg from which all matter and all being is hatched at the beginning of time.

These varying conceptions of Thoth and his origins arise both from changes in Egyptian religious thought across time and also from regional differences in religious practices. In the city of Memphis, the supreme god was Ptah, and Thoth was conceptualized as both the tongue and the wisdom of Ptah.[99] The myth of the egg mentioned above, by contrast, comes from the city of Hermopolis, and may have been a later addition to religious doctrine and practice there.[100] Indeed, the very name of Hermopolis is a reference to Thoth. The original Egyptian name was Khemenu, a reference to the Ogdoad, or Eight Gods, that were worshiped in that city, but when Egypt was Hellenized, the name was changed to Hermopolis, which literally means "City of Hermes" in Greek. This change came about because of the syncretization of the Greek god Hermes with Thoth and because of the central importance of Thoth to Egyptian religious practice in Hermopolis.

In all parts of Egypt, Thoth was considered to be a lunar god. One myth explains that Thoth acquired his association with the moon when the heavily pregnant goddess Nut asked him for help in reversing the curse placed on her by Ra, who had told her that she would not be able to give birth during any day on the calendar, which at that time had 360 days. Thoth solves the problem by gambling with the moon god Khonsu, setting the stakes at a fifth of Khonsu's light. When Thoth wins the contest, he uses Khonsu's light to create five intercalary days, during which Nut is finally able to give birth to Osiris, Horus, Set, Isis, and Nephthys. In this myth, we also see Thoth's role as a god of time and the calendar, since it is his bet with Khonsu that allows the calendar to be expanded from the lunar 360 days to the solar 365. Thoth therefore is responsible for ensuring that the seasons and the calendar remain aligned.

Thoth was credited with inventing the art of writing, and in this capacity he was especially revered by the scribes of ancient Egypt. Because of this association with words and writing, Thoth was depicted as the recorder of human deeds who stood with Anubis beside the scales that weighed human hearts after death in order to determine the soul's ultimate eternal fate. In other contexts, Thoth

[99] Ions, Egyptian Mythology, 28.
[100] Ions, Egyptian Mythology, 29.

uses his skills with writing and his wisdom to function as a scribe, herald, and judge for the supreme god Ra and the other deities. We see this in the New Kingdom myth "The Battle of Horus and Set," summarized in the chapter on Horus above. When Ra desires to send letters to various gods and goddesses, it is Thoth who takes dictation from Ra and sends the letters. In this story, Thoth also makes performative proclamations instituting the commands of various deities. When Thoth makes statements such as "Let this thing be done!" he functions both as a judge who determines whether laws are to be enacted and as a herald who announces the start of a new law.

During the Ptolemaic Period, Thoth was absorbed into Greek and Roman religion, where he was syncretized with the Greek god Hermes, as mentioned earlier, and with the Roman god Mercury. Like Thoth, Hermes was associated with writing and was considered to be the messenger or herald of the Olympian gods. Thoth also acquired Hermes's role as the guide of souls into the Underworld, and became known as "Hermes Trismegistus," or "Thrice-Great Hermes."

As Hermes Trismegistus, Thoth was credited with having written a series of books on magic, known collectively as the *Corpus Hermeticum,* or "Body of Works by Hermes." These texts were, in fact, written by an anonymous human author during the second century CE and not by Thoth himself, but the association with the god granted the *Corpus* a certain cachet among magicians and seekers after truth. The *Corpus* was also incredibly important to Renaissance and Early Modern magicians and was a focal text in the practice of alchemy, a magical science that laid some of the important groundwork for modern chemistry.

Interest in Thoth's magic was revived in the late nineteenth and early twentieth centuries by groups such as the Hermetic Order of the Golden Dawn, a secret group interested in magic and the occult whose membership included Irish revolutionary Maud Gonne and authors Sir Arthur Conan Doyle, W. B. Yeats, and Bram Stoker. One other member of the Order was the occultist Aleister Crowley, whose *Book of Thoth* is an essay on the history and uses of the tarot deck that draws on aspects of various ancient religions and mythologies, including those of Egypt. Crowley especially connects Thoth with the tarot figure of the Juggler (also known in the modern tarot as the Magician), which Crowley considered to be aligned with Mercury, both the planet and the Roman god.

The Tuat (Duat)

The Tuat was the ancient Egyptian Underworld, and it had multiple functions within Egyptian religion and culture. Some functions were cosmological, but most of them related to beliefs about death and to funerary practices. The Tuat was the place where people initially went when they died. It was the domain of Osiris, and it was where the hearts of the dead were weighed to see whether they were pure and clean and thus worthy of paradise or not. The Tuat was also the place that the sun god had to traverse each night as he went from west to east to begin a new day, and it was the place to which the stars descended when their season in the sky was done.

For both human beings and the sun god Ra, the Tuat was a conduit to rebirth, not a final resting place. Ancient Egyptians believed that when the sun descended below the western horizon at night, it entered into the Tuat. When the sun god entered the Tuat as Atum-Ra, the body of the god was separated from his *ba,* or soul, and the body was cast aside and discarded. The sun god therefore needed to be united with a new body and rejuvenated before he could rise again in the east as Khepera, the scarab beetle who pushed the sun up into the sky out of the waters of Nun.

The sun's barge was sometimes known as the Atet boat or the Barque of Millions of Years, but when it went into the Underworld, it was renamed the Meseket boat or Sektet boat. Because there was no wind in the Tuat, the barge had to be rowed or towed along the path between the western entrance and the eastern exit. The work of towing or rowing was done by different sets of deities, depending on where along the path the boat happened to be at the moment. The sun god was always a passenger, and only helped with the journey by speaking to the different beings encountered in the Tuat.

When a human being died, their soul went down into the Tuat, where it had to make its way to the place where the god Anubis weighed the hearts of the dead. If the heart of the dead person was found to be pure and good, the person would leave the Tuat and go to the Field of Reeds, which was the Egyptian paradise. In the Field of Reeds, the dead person was reunited with their body, and they continued to live in much the same way as they had done before death, only without pain, disease, hunger, or hard work. If the heart was found to be evil, however, the soul was devoured by Ammit and destroyed forever, never to be reunited with the body.

The ancient Egyptian fascination with the Tuat and the afterlife is manifest in the hundreds of surviving funerary texts that describe the Tuat's hazards, denizens, and geographical features. Such texts also provided spells and other information the soul of the dead person would need to navigate the dangers of the Tuat. At first, funerary texts were written only in the tombs of the pharaohs, because it was believed that only the pharaoh was able to go on to paradise and live forever. Later, this privilege was accorded to the nobility, but eventually any Egyptian person was thought to be eligible for resurrection and eternal life in the Field of Reeds. This doctrinal change created a market for funerary texts, which would be buried with the mummified body for the use of the dead person as they made their way across the Tuat.

Funerary texts became available to anyone with the funds to purchase them starting in the New Kingdom. Two of the most important texts were the *Book of the Dead* and the *Amduat*. The latter is a lavishly illustrated book whose title literally means "what is in the Underworld," and it gives a detailed description of the sun's nighttime journey. The *Book of the Dead*, by contrast, is less a description of the Underworld than a practical guide to how to get through it.

According to the *Amduat*, the Tuat was divided into twelve regions, with each region representing one of the twelve hours of the night. Each region has its own geographical features and is inhabited by its own set of deities, some of whom temporarily join Ra's crew in order to get his barge from one end of the region to the other. One such deity who is aboard only through a particular region is called the "Lady of the Boat"; her duty is to protect Ra and his barge while it is in her territory. In addition to deities and various physical features, some regions also have hazards that need to be negotiated. The solar barge itself undergoes changes depending on where it happens to be at the moment. For example, the mummified Ra is usually seated either in an open space in the middle of the boat or else under a kind of tent, but at one point a friendly giant serpent comes aboard and forms a new tent with its body to protect Ra on that part of his journey.

Below are highly abbreviated descriptions of the twelve regions according to the *Amduat*:[101]

> 1.   In one illustration for this region, the sun god stands in the middle of the barge in his *ba*-form as a ram-headed man with a solar disk between his horns; in another, he is shown as a scarab beetle. Egyptologist Erik Hornung states that this is intended to show that the sun's journey is expected to be completed successfully.[102] Nine baboons in this region have the

---

[101] Synopsis based on E. A. Wallace Budge, *The Egyptian Heaven and Hell,* vol. 1: *The Book Am-Tuat* (London: Kegan Paul, Trench, Trübner & Co., Ltd., 1905); Erik Hornung, *The Ancient Egyptian Books of the Afterlife,* trans. David Lorton (Ithaca: Cornell University Press, 1999), 33–53; and Remler, *Egyptian Mythology A to Z,* 9.

[102] Hornung, Books of the Afterlife, 34.

job of opening the gates of the Tuat so that the solar barge can go through, while another nine sing to Ra. Because the sun is dead and has no light at this point, there are magical serpents who provide light in this region. Various other deities praise the sun god, who asks permission to enter the Tuat proper. Permission is granted, and the baboons open the doors.

2.   Still in his ram-headed form (which with one exception he will keep until the end of the journey), the sun god rides in his barge along a stream. Several rowers propel the barge. Isis and Nephthys are aboard in the form of serpents. Ra's boat is accompanied by several other barges at this stage. One is the barge of the moon, another is the barge of Hathor, a third is occupied by a god in lizard form, and the last is the boat of Neper, the god of grain, who is an avatar of Osiris. Many other gods and goddesses are in this region as well, who praise Ra and ask him to renew himself. Ra replies with blessings for the denizens of the region and a command that evil beings be banished. He then asks for help in his journey across the Tuat.

3.   The barge is rowed along with ram-headed Ra in the middle. As in the second region, there are four other boats on the river with the solar barge. The first is called "the boat that capsizes," and it carries Horus deities. The second and third boats are called "the boat of rest" and "the boat of the branch," respectively. Each carries a mummified Osiris. In addition to the main deity, each of these subsidiary boats have a crew of other gods and goddesses. Mummified forms of Osiris appear elsewhere in the illustrations for this region as well.

4.   In the fourth region, water does not flow. The barge instead has to be towed over sand, and it is a different barge from the one in the first three regions, having serpents' heads at the prow and stern. The fourth region is called the "region of Sokar." Sokar (or Seker) was the Memphite god of the dead. Snakes slither over the sand here, and instead of moving

straight across the page, the solar boat now takes a downward path, which goes from the upper right corner to the lower left. One part of the illustration shows two gods guarding the Eye of Ra. In Wallace Budge's edition of the book, these gods are Thoth and Horus. The winged sun disk appears in this region as well, as does the goddess Maat.

5.   Still in the region of Sokar, Ra's boat continues its descent, this time moving diagonally downward from the upper left corner to the lower right. The burial mound of Osiris is here, watched over by Isis and Nephthys, who are in bird-form as kites. Ra makes various addresses to the beings who live in this region, asking that he be allowed to pass through unmolested.

6.   Ra switches to a barge that floats on the water and is paddled by a crewman. Erik Hornung states that this water is the water of Nun.[103] There are four sets of mummified beings, and each set represents the kings of a different cardinal direction. The dead body of Ra is represented by a recumbent man holding the scarab of Khepera over his head, encircled by an enormous serpent. According to Hornung, it is in this region that the dead body of the sun is conceptualized as the dead body of Osiris, which here is reunited with its *ba*, represented by the scarab.

7.   The seventh region is called the "Hall of Osiris." Ra is once again depicted as a ram-headed man with the solar disk between his horns, but instead of the usual canopy, he is now covered by an arch made by the giant serpent Mehen. Mehen will continue to protect Ra in this way until Ra is reborn as Khepera and rises as the new sun. Isis stands in the prow with her arms outstretched, using her magic to make the boat move. The giant serpent Apophis is shown having been defeated; his body is pierced by six knives, while a goddess strangles him

---

[103] Hornung, Books of the Afterlife, 37.

near his head and a god ties up his tail. A form of Horus also appears in this region, in the form of a seated man with a hawk's head, on which is the solar disk to which a *uraeus* is attached. It is Horus's job to make the stars rise and to see to it that time continues to flow. Twelve gods represent the stars, while twelve goddesses represent the hours of the day and night.

8.   In this region, Mehen's power gives the crew towing the barge the ability to make progress across the waters. There are four rams depicted here, each with a different headdress. The rams represent manifestations of Tatanen, the god of the primordial mound from which creation arose. Several other deities are depicted along with looms and other things needed to weave cloth. Of these representations of weaving, Erik Hornung observes that "[t]he theme of this hour is thus the supplying of clothes, which from early times on represented a high priority among the things wished for in the afterlife."[104]

9.   One section of the illustrations for this region shows the twelve gods who row Ra's barge. The other job these gods have is to use their paddles to splash water onto the riverbank for the use of the spirits who dwell there. Ra also promises to provide food and drink for the beings who live in this region. Besides the crew of the barge, there are twelve goddesses who sing praises to Osiris, and twelve fire-breathing *uraei* who use their power to protect Ra as he passes by.

10.   Ra continues to stand under the arch of Mehen's body, but now he carries an ankh in his right hand, while his left holds a staff in the shape of a serpent. A series of illustrations show four gods holding spears, four holding arrows, and four holding bows. Ra bids these gods destroy his enemies with their weapons. The spirits of those who have drowned dwell in the waters here; Ra promises that they can enter paradise even

---

[104] Hornung, Books of the Afterlife, 39.

though they haven't been mummified. It is in the tenth region that Ra and Khepera are joined together in preparation for sunrise. This is represented in part by an illustration of a scarab beetle pushing an elliptical shape that represents the horizon. Thoth, in his baboon manifestation, holds the Eye of Horus so that it can be healed by the goddess Sekhmet.

11.   The text for this region states that the deities who live here are guiding the sun to the eastern horizon so that he can rise again. Ra rides in his boat covered by Mehen, but elsewhere in this section, Mehen appears as an enormously long snake being carried along by twelve gods who go on foot. Their job is to see to it that Mehen also arrives safely at the eastern horizon. A fourfold manifestation of the goddess Neith is to be found here, as are a series of pits of fire in which the enemies of Ra are consumed. Each pit has its own attendant deity tending the flames.

12.   After a long and dangerous journey, Ra's solar barge finally arrives at the eastern horizon. Ram-headed Ra stands in the middle of the boat under his Mehen-canopy, while Khepera occupies the prow in the form of a scarab. One portion of the text in Budge's translation reads: "Then this great god taketh up his position in the Eastern Horizon of heaven, and Shu receiveth him, and he cometh into being in the East."[105] But before sunrise can happen, Ra's barge has to travel the length of a giant serpent named Ankhneteru. For this part of the journey, the barge is towed by twelve gods and twelve goddesses. The goddesses towing the barge also have the duty of creating breezes on earth. Twelve additional goddesses carry fire-breathing serpents on their shoulders. The serpents use their fire to repel the enemies of Ra, especially the demon serpent Apophis. Another twelve gods sing praises to Ra. The final illustration shows a curved wall at the rightmost edge of the

---

[105] Budge, *Am-Tuat*, 258.

papyrus. This represents the horizon. The god Khepera, in the form of a scarab beetle, pushes the sun disk through the middle of the wall. The disk is placed beneath the head of the air god Shu, whose arms extend along the inner perimeter of the wall. At the bottom of the wall is a mummy representing Ra's night body, which he has cast off and which will be destroyed now that he has been born again as the rising sun.

Here's another book by Matt Clayton
that you might be interested in

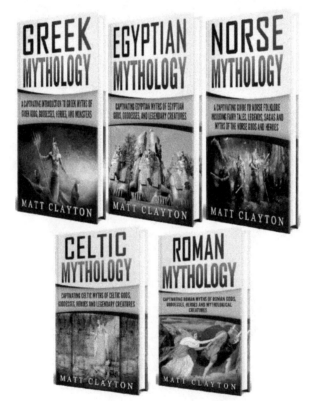

Bibliography

Allen, James P. *The Ancient Egyptian Pyramid Texts*. Atlanta: Society of Biblical Literature, 2005.

Bricault, Laurent. *Isis Pelagia: Images, Names and Cults of a Goddess of the Seas*. Trans. Gil H. Renberg. Leiden: Brill, 2020.

Budge, E. A. Wallace. *Osiris and the Egyptian Resurrection*. 2 vols. London: P. L. Warner, [1911].

——. *The Book of Opening the Mouth: The Egyptian Texts With English Translations*. 2 vols. London: Kegan Paul, Trench, Trübner & Co., Ltd., 1909.

——. *The Egyptian Heaven and Hell*. Vol. 1: *The Book Am-Tuat*. London: Kegan Paul, Trench, Trübner & Co., Ltd., 1905.

Bunson, Margaret. *Encyclopedia of Ancient Egypt*. Rev. ed. New York: Facts on File, Inc., 2010.

Cary, Henry, trans. *Herodotus*. London: George Bell and Sons, 1901.

Crowley, Aleister. *The Book of Thoth*. Repr. York Beach: Samuel Weiser, Inc., 1995.

David, A. Rosalie. *Discovering Ancient Egypt*. New York: Facts on File, Inc., 1994.

——. *The Ancient Egyptians: Religious Beliefs and Practices.* London: Routledge & Kegan Paul, 1982.

Eddy, Paul Rhodes, and Gregory A. Boyd. *The Jesus Legend: A Case for the Historical Reliability of the Synoptic Jesus Tradition.* Grand Rapids: Baker Academic, 2007.

Ellis, Normandi. *Feasts of Light: Celebrations for the Seasons of Life Based on the Egyptian Goddess Mysteries.* Wheaton: The Theosophical Publishing House, 1999.

Escolano-Poveda, Marina. "Imhotep: A Sage Between Fiction and Reality." American Research Center in Egypt website, accessed 23 June 2020, https://www.arce.org/resource/imhotep-sage-between-fiction-and-reality.

Forty, Jo. *Ancient Egyptian Mythology.* Edison: Chartwell Books, Inc., 1996.

Frankfort, Henri. *Ancient Egyptian Religion.* New York: Harper & Row, 1948.

Frazer, James George. *The Golden Bough: A Study in Magic and Religion*, Part IV, Vol. 2, 3rd ed., *Adonis Attis Osiris.* London: The MacMillan Press, Ltd., 1914.

Graves-Brown, Carolyn. *Dancing for Hathor: Women in Ancient Egypt.* London: Continuum, 2010.

Griffiths, John Gwyn. *The Origins of Osiris and his Cult.* Leiden: Brill, 1980.

Hart, George. *A Dictionary of Egyptian Gods and Goddesses.* London: Routledge, 2000.

Heyob, Sharon Kelly. *The Cult of Isis Among Women in the Graeco-Roman World.* Leiden: E. J. Brill, 1975.

Hollis, Susan Tower. *Five Egyptian Goddesses: Their Possible Beginnings, Actions, and Relationships in the Third Millennium BCE.* n.c.: Bloomsbury Publishing, 2019.

Hornung, Erik. *The Ancient Egyptian Books of the Afterlife*. Trans. David Lorton. Ithaca: Cornell University Press, 1999.

Ikram, Salima. "Protecting Pets and Cleaning Crocodiles: The Animal Mummy Project." In *Divine Creatures: Animal Mummies in Ancient Egypt*. Edited by Salima Ikram, 207-27. Cairo: The American University in Cairo Press, 2005.

Ions, Veronica. *Egyptian Mythology*. New York: Peter Bedrick Books, 1990.

Jackson, Leslie. *Isis: The Eternal Goddess of Egypt and Rome*. London: Avalonia, 2016.

King, C. W., trans. *Plutarch's Morals: Theosophical Essays*. London: George Bell & Sons, 1889.

Kramer, Samuel Noah. *Mythologies of the Ancient World*. Garden City: Doubleday, 1961.

Lesko, Leonard H. "Ancient Egyptian Cosmogonies and Cosmology." In *Religion in Ancient Egypt: Gods, Myths, and Personal Practice*, edited by Byron E. Shafer, 90-121. Ithaca. Cornell University Press, 1991.

Lichtheim, Miriam. *Ancient Egyptian Literature: A Book of Readings*. Vol. 3, *The Late Period*. Berkeley: University of California Press, 1980.

——. *Ancient Egyptian Literature: A Book of Readings*. Vol. 2, *The New Kingdom*. Berkeley: University of California Press, 1976.

——. *Ancient Egyptian Literature: A Book of Readings*. Vol. 1, *The Old and Middle Kingdoms*. Berkeley: University of California Press, 1973.

Maehler, Herwig. "Roman Poets on Egypt." In *Ancient Perspectives on Egypt*, ed. by Roger Matthews and Cornelia Roemer, 203-15. London: UCL Press, 2003.

Mark, Joshua J. "Amun." *Ancient History Encyclopedia*, 29 July 2016, https://www.ancient.eu/amun/.

———. "Isis." *Ancient History Encyclopedia*, 19 February 2016, https://www.ancient.eu/isis/.

Martin, Luther H. *Hellenistic Religions: An Introduction*. New York: Oxford University Press 1987.

McCabe, Elizabeth A. *An Examination of the Isis Cult with Preliminary Exploration into New Testament Studies*. Lanham: University Press of America, Inc., 2008.

Mercer, Samuel A. B. *The Religion of Ancient Egypt*. London: Luzac & Co., Ltd., 1949.

Meyer, Marvin W., ed. *The Ancient Mysteries: A Sourcebook*. San Francisco: Harper & Row, 1987.

Mosjov, Bojana. *Osiris: Death and Afterlife of a God*. Malden: Blackwell Publishing, 2005.

Myśliwiec, Karol. *Eros on the Nile*. Trans. Geoffrey L. Packer. Ithaca: Cornell University Press, 1998.

Piankoff, Alexandre, trans., and Natacha Rambova, ed. *Mythological Papyri: Texts*. New York: Pantheon Books, 1957.

Pinch, Geraldine. *A Handbook of Egyptian Mythology*. Santa Barbara: ABC-CLIO, 2002.

———. *Magic in Ancient Egypt*. London: British Museum Press, 1994.

Quirke, Stephen. *Exploring Religion in Ancient Egypt*. Chichester: John Wiley & Sons, Ltd., 2010.

Regula, de Traci. *The Mysteries of Isis: Her Worship and Magick*. St. Paul: Llewellyn Publications, 2001.

Remler, Pat. *Egyptian Mythology A to Z*. 3rd ed. New York: Chelsea House, 2010.

Roth, Ann Macy. "Fingers, Stars, and the 'Opening of the Mouth': The Nature and Function of the *nṯrwj*-Blades." *Journal of Egyptian Archaeology* 79 (1993): 57–79.

Simpson, William Kelley, ed. *The Literature of Ancient Egypt: An Anthology of Stories, Instructions, Stelae, Autobiographies, and Poetry*. New Haven: Yale University Press, 2003.

Smith, Mark. *Following Osiris: Perspectives on the Osirian Afterlife from Four Millennia*. Oxford: Oxford University Press, 2017.

Smith, Martyn. *Religion, Culture, and Sacred Space*. New York: Palgrave MacMillan, 2008.

Spence, Lewis. *Myths and Legends of Ancient Egypt* (Boston: David D. Nickerson & Co., [1915]).

Tacitus, Cornelius. *The Works of Tacitus: The Oxford Translation, Revised*. Vol. 2: *The History, Germany, Agricola, and Dialogue on Orations*. New York: Harper & Brothers, Publishers, 1858.

Takács, Sarolta A. *Isis and Sarapis in the Roman World*. Leiden: E. J. Brill, 1995.

Tobin, Vincent Arieh. "Isis and Demeter: Symbols of Divine Motherhood." *Journal of the American Research Center in Egypt* 28 (1991): 187–200.

Traunecker, Claude. *The Gods of Egypt*. Trans. David Lorton. Ithaca: Cornell University Press, 2001.

Tripolitis, Antonía. *Religions of the Hellenistic-Roman Age*. Grand Rapids: William B. Eerdmans Publishing Company, 2002.

Van Der Toorn, Karel, et al., eds. *Dictionary of Deities and Demons in the Bible*. 2nd ed. Leiden: Brill, 1999.

Watterson, Barbara. *The Gods of Ancient Egypt*. New York: Facts on File, Inc., 1984.

White, J. E. Manchip. *Ancient Egypt: Its Culture and History*. New York: Dover Publications, 1970.

Wildung, Dietrich. *Egyptian Saints: Deification in Pharaonic Egypt*. New York: New York University Press, 1977.

Witt, R. E. Isis in the Ancient World. Baltimore: Johns Hopkins University Press, 1971.

Barker, William Henry, and Cecilia Sinclair. West African Folk-Tales. London: G. G. Harrap & Company, 1917.

Bishop, Herbert L. "A Selection of SiRonga Folklore." South African Journal of Science 19 (1922): 383-400.

Callaway, Henry. Nursery Tales, Traditions, and Histories of the Zulus, in their own *Words*. Springvale, Natal: J. A. Blair, 1868.

Ceni, A. *African Folktales*. Trans. Elizabeth Leister. n. c.: Barnes & Noble, Inc., 1998.

Chatelain, Heli. *Folk-Tales of Angola*. Boston: Houghton Mifflin, 1894.

Cole, Joanna. *Best-Loved Folktales of the World*. Garden City: Doubleday & Company, 1982.

Courlander, Harold. *The Hat-Shaking Dance and Other Ashanti Tales from Ghana*. New York: Harcourt, Brace & World, Inc., 1957.

Dennett, R. E. *Notes on the Folklore of the Fjort (French Congo)*. Publications of the Folk-Lore Society, vol. 41. London: David Nutt, 1898.

Garner, Alan. *The Guizer: A Book of Fools*. New York: Greenwillow Books, 1976.

Lang, Andrew, ed. *The Grey Fairy Book*. London: Longmans, Green, and Co., 1905.

Lester, Julius. *How Many Spots Does a Leopard Have? and Other Tales*. New York: Scholastic, Inc., 1989.

——. *Black Folktales*. New York: Richard W. Baron, 1969.

Littman, Enno. *Publications of the Princeton Expedition to Abyssinia*. Vol. 2. Leyden: E. J. Brill, 1910.

Lynch, Patricia Ann. *African Mythology A to Z*. New York: Facts on File, Inc., 2004.

Mayo, Isa Fyvie. *Old Stories and Sayings of the Continent of Africa*. London: C. W. Daniel, n.d.

Radin, Paul, ed. *African Folktales.* Princeton: Princeton University Press, 1970.

Riley, Dorothy Winbush. *The Complete Kwanzaa: Celebrating our Cultural Harvest.* New York: HarperPerennial, 1995.

Scheub, Harold. *African Tales.* Madison: University of Wisconsin Press, 2005.

Stumme, Hans. *Märchen und Gedichte aus der Stadt Tripolis in Nordafrika.* Leipzig: J. C. Hinrichs'sche Buchhandlung, 1898.

Theall, George McCall. *Kaffir Folk-Lore.* London: Swan Sonnenschein, Le Bas & Lowrey, 1886.

Tremearne, A. J. N. *Hausa Superstitions and Customs: An Introduction to the Folk-Lore and the Folk.* London: J. Bale, Sons & Danielson, Ltd., 1913.

Tyler, Josiah. *Forty Years Among the Zulus.* Boston: Congregational Sunday-School and Pub. Society, 1891.

CPSIA information can be obtained
at www.ICGtesting.com
Printed in the USA
LVHW041724231020
669603LV00005B/79